—Navigating the—
PANDEMIC

Stories of Hope and Resilience

Edited by

Teresa Schreiber Werth

PAGE PUBLISHING, INC.
Conneaut Lake, PA

First originally published by Page Publishing 2021

ISBN 978-1-6624-2469-4 (pbk)
ISBN 978-1-6624-2470-0 (digital)

Printed in the United States of America

For Amanda and Adam

In praise of NAVIGATING THE PANDEMIC: Stories of Hope and Resilience

This timely collection of essays, memoirs, and poems rises out of the professional insights and lived experiences of its authors who address the pain of grief, loss, and racism seen through the lens of the COVID-19 pandemic. Middle-aged, old, and young voices tell their inspiring stories and provide candid looks at real situations. They share their pain—and the wisdom they have found on the other side of pain—and offer practical advice for not only persevering, but thriving. Here you will find testimonies of resilience, gratitude, and hope. Read them one a day, to strengthen our resolve to re-envision ourselves and our lives together, to build empathy and solidarity, and to create a "brave new space" where every person can choose life!

— Kay Kupper Berg, M.A., retired Professor of English,
Sinclair Community College, Dayton, Ohio

The personal stories that emerged as the world navigated the Covid-19 virus pandemic will be valuable to future generations in understanding the toll taken on so many who, though sheltering in isolation, were not alone in their experiences. As the end to many others' stories have not yet appeared while this virus continues to rage on, comfort can be found knowing we're not solitary in just our confusion and our fears, but also in our hope. This compilation of narratives will ring with familiarity to the struggles of many, while the professional guidance offered will help to inform as we move forward. Overall, this book emphasizes the importance of reaching out, while holding on.

— Penny Simonson is a freelance writer, public speaker and artist who makes her home in Spokane Valley, Washington

Years from now, what will you tell your grandchildren about the pandemic of 2020? Your memories plus the voices of over 30 women and men in *Navigating the Pandemic* show how the human mind, body and spirit can cope with the concurrent traumas of a deadly pandemic and racial injustice. These essays and poems will renew your faith that we *can* endure and overcome adversity.

— Norma Press, Author and Editor

Contents

Foreword

Timothy Quill, MD

To put it mildly, we live in strange and unsettling times. To some degree things have been this way for a long time, but the coronavirus epidemic and the murder of George Floyd have brought the vulnerable, unraveling, unsettling aspects of our lives and our world into sharp relief. Our usual cultural rituals for responding to these losses have been turned on their head with coronavirus and with our awakening to the terrible disparities in our midst, compounding our losses and aggravating our isolation and, at times, despair. As we search to make sense of the associated uncertainty and loss, perhaps now more on our own than ever, we struggle to find community with others who may be having similar experiences.

Teresa Schreiber Werth, a certified funeral celebrant (CFC), is no stranger to grief and loss. Her work includes counseling and supporting surviving friends and relatives of the dead in our midst. Her new book entitled *Navigating the Pandemic: Stories of Hope and Resilience* is a collection of short essays written by a diverse group of authors from a wide range of backgrounds about how they, as individuals, have responded to these and other losses in their lives. The essays in the book clearly acknowledge and explore many kinds of loss and how we internalize them as sometimes subtle layers of grief, but they also provide breaths of fresh air and honesty in these unnerving times. While the traditional understanding of grief is explored, no overly simplified formula is presented. Yet seeing such a diverse array of responses may open doors for some and, for others, simply provide comfort in knowing we are not alone in these challenging times.

Timothy E. Quill, MD, is retired professor of medicine, psychiatry, medical humanities, and nursing at the University of Rochester Medical Center. He is a palliative care physician, author, educator, scholar, and advocate. He was past president of the American Academy of Hospice and Palliative Medicine. His latest book, *Voluntarily Stopping Eating and Drinking: A Compassionate, Widely Available Option for Hastening Death,* will be released later this year by Oxford University Press.

Acknowledgments

I first reached out to my funeral celebrant friends, asking them to write stories to help those faced with loved ones dying alone, funerals denied or delayed, and the many new kinds of grief people were experiencing at the start of the pandemic in the United States. I also asked my longtime friend and author, David Seaburn, to join me in writing. Dave's response to my invitation was not what I expected. He liked my idea, but he wanted more specifics about the topics, the project's scope, and the new landscapes of grief that I was proposing we explore. He suggested I first needed to connect with some mental health professionals and frontline workers.

Dave shared a blog with me, written by Andrew Penn, MS, NP, about the very topic I wanted to explore: navigating the emotions of a pandemic. I reached out to Andrew, and overnight—in the space of one e-mail—inspiration arrived! Andrew's expertise helped me to better understand the many ways the pandemic was creating new types of loss and layers of grief. He helped me to see some of the unique ways people were being affected. I realized that within communities and subcultures, there were important stories, and I set out to write them or find people who would.

As I look now at the list of writers, the stories, and the poems in this book, what I see, besides authentic sharing of the pandemic's impact on people's lives, is the culmination of a lifetime of networking. I see people I have known for decades as colleagues and friends, like Julia Hahn, my first editor, who accepted the task of editing many of the stories. I see Ginny Cross, Maria Delgado-Sutton, and Gloria Osborne, who were always available as sounding boards to provide encouragement, to read drafts, and to offer suggestions. They helped me stay focused on the mission of storytelling that would be hopeful and resilient as well as historically accurate and inclusive. Jonna Wing and Cathy Roma identified stories that seemed nothing short of miraculous to me because they connected me with writers I had never met, but very much needed to know. Together, 39 writers have contributed 51 stories and poems telling a much bigger story than just America's experience of coronavirus. They tell how the pandemic has impacted other parts of the world as well. Each writer offers intimate glimpses into their own experiences and expertise for which I am eternally grateful.

I am grateful to Tim Quill, MD, who took time away from completing his own book to write a thoughtful foreword for mine. Our work has produced a not-for-profit project whose net proceeds will be donated to the Society of Refugee Healthcare Providers (www. refugeesociety.org).

My husband of 49 years, Don, has always been my biggest fan. It is to him I owe the most thanks for enabling me to spend my pandemic isolation at my computer, reaching out, gathering in, and building a book that is designed to be a tool to inspire and to help heal. I hope it will also be seen as an accurate and insightful historical record of much that has happened between the start of the pandemic and the first half of 2020.

Finally, to you, the reader, thank you for whatever brings you to this place. In some ways, I believe this is a sacred place holding lives lived and lives lost, lives now bound to COVID-19.

Introduction

Pictures can be powerful communicators. You can probably recall iconic images that define a specific moment in time: the World Trade Center buildings collapsing, the Kennedys hunched over in the car in Dallas after the shooting, the Challenger spacecraft exploding, the rubble in Puerto Rico after Hurricane Maria, and the lava flows after the volcanic eruptions in Hawaii—strong, vivid, unforgettable images. For me and COVID-19, it was the picture of the refrigerator trucks in the parking lot of Elmhurst Hospital in Queens, New York, in mid-March 2020. That's the image that first put me over the edge.

As a certified funeral celebrant, I could only wonder *who was helping the survivors* of those in the refrigerator trucks? Who was sitting down with them to acknowledge their grief, to comfort them, and to plan for memorial services and celebrations of life or whatever their culture or religion did at the time of death? In the frantic rush to attend to the living, what was happening to the *survivors* of the dead? And what exactly could they be *doing* to respond to their loss?

The circumstances of death for so many, during this pandemic, create new and painful situations with which few of us have ever had to deal. The very nature of the pandemic demands harsh separation between the sick and the healthy for the good of both. But when we are denied the most basic end-of-life comforts—to be at the bedside of the dying, to hug and kiss and hold hands, to sit for long hours, to pray and

17

read and sing, to witness the last breath, and to have our hearts broken—when we are denied those moments and those memories, we are lost.

Some of these pages are written for those people who now find themselves lost because their loved one died alone. Other pages are written for the rest of us and the many new types of grief and loss we all are experiencing. We reach out to you with ideas about what you can be doing today:

- if you could not be or cannot be with a loved one who is dying,
- if a funeral or memorial service must be postponed,
- if you are exhausted by uncertainty, grief, and many new types of loss, or
- if you are feeling hopeless and helpless in the face of these unfamiliar circumstances.

Everything we have lost, collectively and personally, translates to feelings of grief. We have lost the freedom to congregate, worship, shop, dine, travel, work, play, hug, or shake hands. Gone are our peace of mind and our sense of hope. Some of us have lost our sense of humor. There are aspects of this challenge for which technology offers some new options, but even 21st century technology cannot compensate for hugs and handshakes. The losses created by this pandemic require us to be patient, innovative, flexible, collaborative, resourceful, and most of all, human.

And while it is true that the coronavirus does not discriminate when it comes to age, gender, ethnicity, or borders, it is clearly impacting some communities more than others: the elderly, people of color, the homeless, the undocumented, the incarcerated, the

LGBTQ community, and Indigenous people. Within these pages, you will find stories from those communities that demonstrate the power of faith, cultural wisdom, and survival skills.

Then on May 25, the dynamics of this invisible pandemic shifted mightily with the murder of George Floyd. Out of this tragic incident erupted another whole "dis-ease" for our country: the undeniable injustices and disparities of structural racism and the awakening of all of us to what life is like for Black and brown people in America today. Suddenly, we are all caught in the crosshairs of remaining safe and silent, seeming not to care, or risking our health and safety by joining peaceful protests or other public gatherings bearing witness to our concern and support.

These two crises—of health and humanity—are now inextricably linked in American history. These stories are intended to offer some insight into how we can cope and how we are coping. They are not solutions. They are guideposts. They expose the very crack in humanity that offers us a reset.

In the words of Charles Eisenstein, "A million forking paths lie before us…totalitarianism or solidarity; medical martial law or a holistic renaissance; greater fear of the microbial world or greater resilience as we participate in it; permanent norms of social distancing or a renewed desire to come together… Already we can feel the power of who we might become… No longer the vassals of fear, we can bring order to the kingdom and build an intentional society on the love already shining through the cracks of the world of separation." (Excerpted from "The Coronation" by Charles Eisenstein, March 2020)

Where we go from here really is up to each of us.

Teresa Schreiber Werth

We are the ship. We are the sea.
I sail in you. You sail in me.
Ring all the bells that still can ring.
Forget the perfect offering.
There is a crack in everything.
That's how the Light gets in.

Excerpts from "Somos El Barco" by Lorre Wyatt and "Anthem" by Leonard Cohen

About the Writers

Lynn M. Acquafondata is a licensed mental health counselor and owner of Crossbridge Counseling and Crossbridge Wellness in Rochester, New York. She specializes in grief, family conflict, and spiritual issues. She is an ordained clergyperson and previously worked as a hospice chaplain.

Mara Ahmed is a Pakistani American activist, artist, and independent filmmaker. She was born in Lahore, Pakistan. Her deeply formative migration pathway has informed her practice and has helped her develop a body of work that addresses notions of history, heritage, and tradition. Deeply connected with her roots and in constant dialogue with her contemporaneity and the political moment, Ahmed's work creates art that subverts boundaries and connects different cultures with the universality of her topics. In conjunction with her production company, Neelum Films, Mara has written and directed three documentaries: "The Muslims I Know," "Pakistan One on One," and "A Thin Wall." She is currently working on "The Injured Body," a documentary about racism in America, focusing exclusively on the voices of women of color. Mara's artwork is described by the artist as a multimedia fusion of collage work, photography, graphic art, and film. (Claudia Pretelin, in Instruments of Memory: Conversations with Women in the Arts)

Elizabeth Alexander grew up in the Carolinas and Appalachian Ohio and now makes her home in Saint Paul, Minnesota. Her love of music, language, and challenging questions is reflected in her catalog of over 100 songs and choral pieces in a wide variety of classical and vernacular styles. She earned her doctorate in music composition at Cornell University. Elizabeth's many commissions have included works for orchestra, chamber ensembles, solo instruments, and voice, but she is best known for her choral pieces, which have been performed by thousands of choruses worldwide. When she's not composing music, Elizabeth makes pretty good biscuits, looks for all kinds of excuses to visit her two grown sons, and gardens during the three-month period in Minnesota that is not winter. "No Other People's Children" is a song of reconciliation affirming the "belovedness" of all people. Her work is copyrighted and used with kind permission.

Joyce Arnold is a proficient writer, living in Spencerport, New York. She has participated in writing classes through Osher Lifelong Learning Institute, offering noncredit courses with no assignments or grades to adults over age 50. Her favorite classes have been fiction and memoir writing. Her work also appears in an anthology entitled *Storytelling Around the Table* (2018). She writes, "I like to look closer at life, to zero in at times, to taste it, see it more clearly, to use all my senses to immerse myself in its wonder and yes at times, the pain. These past months, our world, not just MY space, but the world, has experienced fear and uncertainty of the future. When invited to write about my experience of the pandemic, I immediately turned to humor, not to avoid the very real discomfort of life but to stir the optimism in my soul. I believe that the world has yet to see all the good in our hearts and all the good we can do as human beings, in our skins of different shades with the universal language of love and yes, our smiles."

Ysaye Marie Barnwell is a native New Yorker now living in Washington DC. In addition to her degrees in speech pathology and public health and several honorary doctorates, she was a professor of dentistry at Howard University and a sign language interpreter. In 1979 she joined Sweet Honey in the Rock and composed, sang, and recorded with them for 34 years. She has spent many years offstage as a master teacher and choral clinician in African American cultural performance. Her work is copyrighted and used with kind permission.

Guy L. Banks (Tron) has been an entertainer for decades; however, he seeks to contribute more than music, poetry, acting, and his underlying 14-year prison sentence to society. Although his incarceration was designed to be a setback, he has made significant cognitive improvements that have developed him into a public speaker, mentor, program facilitator, producer, poet, and rap artist whom many consider a threat. The 35-year-old father of two daughters from Columbus, Ohio, wants nothing more than to see poor ghetto communities strengthened and developed by taking ownership of their contributions to hip-hop and the rewards they garner.

Damian Barr is a British writer, columnist, and playwright. He is a fellow of the Royal Society of Arts and host of the Literary Salon at Shoreditch House. He tells stories to help people better understand themselves and others, to ask better questions, not provide easy answers. The *Financial Times* recently described him as a literary impresario. "We all have a story but not everyone gets to tell it. I give as much time as I can to bold charitable organizations working hard to help make our society more equal and books and culture more accessible. I started the writers-in-residence scheme for Gladstone's Library and have supported Brighton Fringe to grow into the UK's second largest arts festival. I helped lead the fight to save Newarthill Library. There's always more to do, especially now." His story in this anthology was first written as a tweet and went viral.

Lauren Benton, MA, LCPC is a therapist at a community mental health center that primarily provides services for low-income and high-risk folks in Central Illinois. She is a wife and a new mom who is consistently trying to find the balance between navigating the world as a queer person/parent and using her privilege to work to dismantle the forces that require this navigation and emotional labor from LGBTQIA+ folks.

Aylannie Campbell is a National Honor Society graduate of the Spencerport High School (New York) class of 2020 where she leaves her legacy of passion, determination, and bravery. Aylannie has been involved in many positive activities in her school and community, such as volunteering and participating in her school's sports teams. As the former president of the class of 2020 and president of the student organization DASH2Change (Declare Action to Shift Humanity), she has shown consistent leadership and advocacy despite all odds. Her dream is to change the world and she will do so by continuing to advocate for equity and systematic change for people of color. Aylannie aspires to be a civil rights attorney and is attending the University at Albany for political science.

Cecile Carson is a physician and spiritual counselor who has worked with people facing life-threatening illness for over 30 years. She taught at the University of Rochester School of Medicine from 1977 to 2008, focusing much of her teaching on expanding existing models of health care to address the soul's response to illness in respectful and appropriate forms.

Virginia Cross, RN, MSN, MA is a retired teacher, nurse, and pastor living in Hamlin, New York. She has a lifetime commitment to serving people who are marginalized, beginning with living and teaching in Papua New Guinea. She worked as a nurse practitioner at Anthony Jordan Health Center and served as a hospital chaplain at the University of Rochester Medical Center, as a nurse and chaplain at the Women's Correctional Facility in Albion, New York, and as a nurse at Park Ridge Chemical Dependency Inpatient Unit in Rochester, New York. She now enjoys the outdoors with her husband, family, and new puppy. She seeks beauty and joy each day especially in these challenging times.

Jillian Harrison-Jones is from Rochester, New York. She is the music director for MUSE, Cincinnati's Women's Choir and director of choirs at the historic Witherspoon Presbyterian Church of Indianapolis, Indiana. She is also a fourth-year doctoral student in choral conducting at the University of Cincinnati College-Conservatory of Music (CCM), currently writing her dissertation on effective virtual concert planning amid the COVID-19 pandemic. Jillian earned a bachelor of arts degree in history from Lincoln University, Pennsylvania, a bachelor of music degree from Roberts Wesleyan College, New York, and a master of music degree in choral conducting from the University of Connecticut. Previous appointments include being the Richard Wesp assistant conductor of the Cincinnati Children's Choir, adjunct professor of music at Thomas More University (Kentucky), assistant conductor of the Willimantic Orchestra (Connecticut), and assistant director of the UConn Women's Choir (Connecticut).

Jillian has tremendous experience with children's, women's, and collegiate choirs and orchestras. As an author, clinician, singer, vocal coach, and conductor, Jillian's expertise is in the performance practice and scholarship of African American spiritual and gospel music and devotes her career to redeeming the forgotten and lesser-known choral works of African American composers, such as Glenn Burleigh, Undine Smith Moore, Robert Nathaniel Dett, and more. Jillian is the coauthor of Amazon's best seller entitled *Empower Now for Women* and is married to philanthropist and theologian, Reverend Dr. Winterbourne Harrison-Jones, senior pastor of Witherspoon Presbyterian Church and board president of the Asante Children's Theatre of Indianapolis, Indiana.

Micky ScottBey Jones, the Justice Doula, is an author, speaker, facilitator, and the Director of Healing and Resilience Initiatives with the Southern-based collective, Faith Matters Network, and an Associate Fellow of Racial Justice with Evangelicals for Social Action. Find her on Twitter at @iammickyjones.

Emily Kedar is a psychotherapist and writer based in Toronto and Salt Spring Island, Canada. She arranges words to usher in awe and appreciation of beauty and of pain. Her work can be found in *Acta Victoriana, The Hart House Review,* and *The Bones Behind Her Smile:*

A Kensington Collection. She is also the winner of the 2008 CBC Poetry Face-Off.

Nancy Kennedy lives in Inverness, Florida, and is a staff writer for *Citrus County Chronicle.* Excerpts were taken from her article by the same name appearing in the April 9, 2020, edition of the *Citrus County Chronicle* and used with kind permission.

J. Dawn Knickerbocker belongs to the Anishinaabe people and is a citizen of White Earth Nation and an enrolled member of the Minnesota Chippewa Tribe from the Otter Tail Pillager band of Indians. She is an environmentalist, activist, and "indigi-feminist" working on culturally based sustainable development issues and decolonization in her community. Dawn resides in Yellow Springs, Ohio, with her husband and four sons and is currently a board member of the Greater Cincinnati Native American Coalition and cofounder of WARN (Women of All Red Nations) Ohio.

Adam J. Lazarus is a New York native who grew up in Florida and is now living in Tucson, Arizona. He has been writing fun, funny, and fantastical poems for 25 years and loves to share his unique poetry style and general weirdness with the whole world. He graduated from the University of Florida and primarily works as a digital marketing strategy consultant and content creator for start-ups, e-commerce brands, and evolving digital businesses, but poetry is his passion. As a proud father and family man, Adam tries to find the humor in all things, and his goal, poetically, is to make people laugh, to focus on the lighter side of life, and to help them look at the world a little

differently, hopefully for the better! Check out his website, www.
adamspoems.com, for more cheerful rhymes for challenging times.

Brian Linden is a Chicago native who began working with CBS News
in 1984. From 1984 to 1987, he was involved in interviews with
Chinese leaders (including Deng Xiaoping) and also found time to
play the leading role in a feature-length movie produced by Beijing
Film Studio. He completed his graduate studies at the University
of Illinois, Hopkins-Nanjing Center, and Stanford. He worked on
education investment/development projects in over 75 countries
before returning to China in 2004 to become the first foreigner to
preserve and redevelop a nationally protected Chinese structure now
known as the Linden Centre. Brian and his wife, Jeanee, now have
seven similar projects throughout Yunnan. Each site focuses on the
preservation of existing important historical buildings while incor-
porating the villagers in the planning and management of the final
product—a heritage hotel. The hotels, which consistently are ranked
by Tripadvisor among the top five in all of China, serve as the social
enterprise component that allows them to focus their passions on the
preservation of the social and cultural resources—the "software"—of
the surrounding areas. Their model has been praised by the Chinese
Ministry of Foreign Affairs, the US Secretary of State, and dozens of
media and scholars. Brian's first book will be released in Chinese and
English in early 2021.

Steve McAlpin is a 26-year Army veteran having served in Bosnia and
Afghanistan. He is using this pandemic time to complete writing his
memoirs and to connect with other veterans. He makes his home in
Rochester, New York.

Pennie Sue Williams McGanty is an elementary school teacher in the Virginia Beach City Public Schools system. She has a bachelor's degree in interdisciplinary studies and a master's degree in elementary education, both from Norfolk State University.

Kitty O'Meara has worked as a copywriter and editor, a middle school teacher, and a spiritual care provider in hospital and hospice settings and has always been a writer. She shares her photos and musings about life on her blog, The Daily Round. Her piece "In the Time of Pandemic" resonated with and was shared by people around the world early in the pandemic. It has been used as lyrics for several choral and solo musical settings. It appears here with acknowledgment to Alfred A. Knopf, where it was first published as "And the People Stayed Home" in their book, *Together in a Sudden Strangeness: America's Poets Respond to the Pandemic* (June 2020).

She has created a children's book, *And the People Stayed Home*, released in November 2020, from Tra Publishing (distributed by Simon & Schuster). She is concerned about the effects of this experience (pandemic) on the world's children and the people they will become. She hopes the book will help them "to imagine new stories…and heal themselves and the earth." Her work is copyright protected and used with kind permission.

Gloria Osborne, RN, ADN, BA, aka Grandmother Turtlekneader, is an initiated Grandmother, Reclaiming Witch, Reiki 2 practitioner, holistic nurse, peace activist, and "permaculturist" dedicated to creating tomorrow's dream today through holistic and regenerative practices.

Andrew Penn is a psychiatric nurse practitioner, educator, consultant, and clinician. He is a researcher into the therapeutic use of psychedelic-assisted therapy in psychiatry. Currently, he serves as an associate clinical professor at the University of California-San Francisco School of Nursing and is an attending nurse practitioner at the San Francisco Veterans Administration. As valuable as the pandemic was for getting him to learn how to bake sourdough bread and to play the ukulele, he looks forward to the end of the pandemic when it will be possible to travel the world and hug friends again.

Ida Perez is the director of Ibero Children and Family Stability Services, Scrantom Street Block Club chair, and Poder 97.1 FM radio show host for *Su Hora Informativa* (*Your Informative Hour*) in Rochester, New York.

Catherine Roma (DMA Choral Conducting, College-Conservatory of Music, 1989) believes choral singing is a path to justice, inclusion, and love. Roma is best known as founder and director of Anna Crusis Women's Choir in Philadelphia (1975–1983) and founder and director of MUSE, Cincinnati's Women's Choir for 30 years (1983–2013). Both choirs have exciting and active concert seasons in their respective cities.

Roma recently retired from Wilmington, a small Quaker college, where she was professor of music for 25 years. Through her association with Wilmington College and their commitment to prison education, Roma founded UMOJA Men's Chorus at Warren Correctional Institution in 1993 as part of Wilmington's degree-granting program in prisons in Southwest Ohio.

In retirement Roma founded and conducts the World House Choir, a community arts for justice and peace chorus (2012); UBUNTU Men's Chorus, London Correctional (2012); Hope Thru Harmony Women's Choir, Dayton Correctional (2014); and KUJI Men's Chorus, Marion Correctional (2016).

Roma calls all her choirs choral communities because she believes choral communities inspire, motivate, educate, and heal an ailing world.

David B. Seaburn is a novelist, a retired marriage and family therapist, and a Presbyterian minister. The excerpt in his story is from his novel *Chimney Bluffs* (www.Davidbseaburn.com).

Mara Sapon-Shevin is professor of Inclusive Education, inaugural senior faculty fellow in Diversity and Inclusion, program coordinator in Teaching and Curriculum Doctoral Program, and faculty member in Disability Studies, Women and Gender Studies, and Programs in the Analysis and Resolution of Conflicts and Collaboration at Syracuse University (New York) (www.marasapon-shevin.com).

Marjorie A. Smith, LCSW is currently the executive director of Aurora House Comfort Care Home in Spencerport, New York. She began her career in social work as a therapist working with severely and persistently mentally ill clients. After an enlightening experience with hospice care for her father, she sought a position with a Rochester, New York, hospice agency as a home hospice social worker supporting terminally ill patients and their loved ones and offering a holistic approach to end-of-life care. She is also an ordained wedding officiant.

Teresa Y. Smith, MD, MSEd. is an emergency physician who has dedicated her training to working in the urban communities of New York City. Currently, she serves as the associate dean of graduate medical education and affiliations at SUNY Downstate Health Sciences University, which trains 957 trainees in 51 ACGME-accredited programs. Dr. Smith helped lead the institution through the GME response to the COVID-19 pandemic crisis and, in response to police brutality, helped organize 100+ residents, faculty, and staff in a die-in demonstration to stand up against the health disparities and racial injustice plaguing our country. After completing her undergraduate degree at Spelman College, Dr. Smith attended NYU School of Medicine and finished her training in emergency medicine at NYU Bellevue Hospital. She earned her master's in medical education from the University of Pennsylvania. She served as the previous program director for the Department of Emergency Medicine, which heralds as the largest emergency-medicine training program in the country and a clinical advisory dean for MS4 students in the College of Medicine. Dr. Smith has been an invited speaker on many national and international stages, discussing diversity and inclusion in medicine, women in leadership, and her patient experience. Dr. Smith was recently a Harvard Macy Institute scholar and has been awarded the Dr. Dale Blackstock Award for Excellence in Teaching and Service and GME Program Director Award of Excellence and was named one of the 40 Under 40 Leaders in Minority Health of the National Minority Quality Forum.

Marina Steinke was born and raised in Germany. She and her husband now live in Christchurch, New Zealand. They have three adult children. She was a secondary school teacher for mathematics and physics; software developer; editor of the quarterly publication of the Rare Breeds Conservation Society of New Zealand, *Rare Breeds NewZ*; tutor in adult education; and tour guide. She and her husband grow their own fruits and vegetables and have poultry, alpaca, and sheep to supply them with fibre, eggs, and meat.

James M. Sutton, PA-C is a physician assistant who provides medical care for the homeless in Rochester, New York.

Maria Delgado Sutton has been a nurse for over 32 years with most of her experience in case management of underserved population. For the past 14 years she dedicated her work to help migrant farmworker families seeking solutions to the challenges faced by migrant communities. She is an advocate, mother, and wife and was the primary caregiver for her aging parents before they passed away. Caring for her parents involved long hours and great sacrifice that she purposely chose on behalf of her family.

Ryan R. Tebo was born in Buffalo, New York, in 1974, moved to Stockholm, Sweden, eleven years ago with a Fulbright grant to make a documentary film about American expatriates who settled in Sweden in the 1960s and 1970s, looking for a progressive utopia. Now, in addition to making films, he teaches high school English, digital media, and philosophy in Stockholm. Recently, he began a poetry-reading series in honor of National Poetry Month. His family lives in Lewiston, New York, and Baltimore, Maryland.

Gretchen Volk, MD has been a pediatrician at Westside Pediatrics in Rochester, New York, for the past 18 years. She volunteers regularly with the Glens Falls Medical Mission at a clinic in Nueva Santa Rosa, Guatemala. More of her essays are published by *the Funny Times*.

The Rev. Gordon V. Webster is the current chaplain of the Rochester Presbyterian Home in Rochester, New York. As an ordained Presbyterian minister, he has served four congregations as a pastor; served as a peace mission worker with the Middle East Council of Churches in Beirut, Lebanon; and worked as a founding executive director for both the American Committee for Middle East Dialogue and the Common Good Planning Center of the Rochester Area Community Foundation. He is currently co-president of the American Friends of Oasis of Peace Village in Israel/Palestine. With his family, he created the David Gordon Webster Memorial Trust, whose grants support interfaith and ecumenical work and provide musician/scholar awards at David's high school annually. He is the recipient of the Albert Nelson Marquis Lifetime Achievement Award (2019).

Teresa Schreiber Werth is editor of this anthology, a retired communications professional, freelance writer, editor, author, and funeral and wedding celebrant. Her response to the pandemic has been to write about her observations and experiences during this unprecedented time and to seek out writers from around the United States and the world to tell the human and historic stories about how people are coping with the many new layers of grief and loss we are experiencing as the result of COVID-19.

Bobbi Williams is a spiritual counselor and member of the American Institute of Health Care Professionals and a Usui Reiki master teacher and earned her MBA from the University of Chicago with a behavioral science concentration.

Ayanna Woods is a composer, performer, and bandleader from Chicago. Her music explores the spaces between acoustic and electronic, traditional and esoteric, wildly improvisational and mathematically rigorous.

Camryn Zeitvogel is a member of the class of 2020 who recently graduated from the Aquinas Institute in Rochester, New York. She shares the speech she delivered at her class's baccalaureate service on June 5, 2020. She is presently studying early childhood education and music at Ohio State University. She hopes to someday become a teacher and a pit orchestra musician.

In the Time of Pandemic

Kitty O'Meara

And the people stayed home.

And they listened, and read books, and rested, and exercised, and made art, and played games, and learned new ways of being, and were still.

And they listened more deeply. Some meditated, some prayed, some danced. Some met their shadows. And the people began to think differently.

And the people healed.

And, in the absence of people living in ignorant, dangerous, and heartless ways, the earth began to heal.

And when the danger passed, and the people joined together again, they grieved their losses, and made new choices, and dreamed new images, and created new ways to live and heal the earth fully, as they had been healed.

Our Losses Take Many Forms

Andrew Penn

As a health-care professional, I have watched the progress of the COVID-19 pandemic with alternating measures of horror, dread, fascination, frustration, and fear.

The five stages of grief (denial, anger, bargaining, depression, and acceptance), as outlined by Elizabeth Kübler-Ross to describe the emotional journey of preparing for the death of a loved one, plot a useful map as we transit through the uncharted emotional aspects of the COVID-19 pandemic. Others have added *meaning* as an important sixth step.

For some time, many people, including some in important positions of leadership, appeared to be in denial about the risk of this virus. For many of us, it was an event happening in another part of the world—concerning, of course, but not immediately impactful. We went about our springtime lives, planning conferences, basketball tournaments, and vacations, unaware of what could befall us. Denial always looks foolish in retrospect, but at the time of the threat, denial is adaptive as it permits us to navigate a world of unpredictable threats without becoming paralyzed with fear.

As the threat of the virus came close, our collective anxiety turned to anger and fear of harm and scarcity, which led to absurd behaviors—

hoarding toilet paper or, worse, hand sanitizer and N95 masks. Those conditions led to genuine, appropriate anger as health-care workers were left to improvise personal protective equipment, leading well-intentioned citizens to organize sewing bees to make surgical masks, and we all asked the question, *"Why didn't we start preparing sooner?"*

Anger led to bargaining as we realized the potential harm of this pandemic and the need to enforce social distancing through closure orders of bars and restaurants and, increasingly, shelter-in-place orders that turned some of our largest cities into ghost towns. Stock markets buckled, unemployment claims skyrocketed, and questions began to be asked: Could we still maintain a healthy economy and still contain COVID-19? How many people would we be willing to allow to perish to continue a robust economy?

Indeed, in a time when the pandemic of coronavirus has made shelter-in-place orders essential, everyone and every surface become potential threats. When I walk in my usually bustling San Francisco neighborhood, the streets are eerily quiet, and people cross the street rather than pass on the sidewalk with less than six feet separating us. I come home, wash my hands, and hope that somewhere, somehow, a virus hasn't found its way into my respiratory tract.

At the start of a crisis, anxiety is adaptive because it is hardwired into us to get us to pay attention, to mobilize for action. This energy can only be used for so long to motivate handwashing and house disinfecting before sheer exhaustion sets in. When that begins to occur, the anxiety turns to depression and demoralization as we begin to feel the duration of the threat and the grief that come from not only current losses, but also the *anticipatory anxiety* that stems from not knowing what loss will come next. Sometimes called *ambiguous loss,* it is the sorrow over things that are uncertain and incomplete. Will we not be able to take that trip of a lifetime that we had planned for this summer? Will we see our kids graduate? Or worse, will we lose our jobs and livelihoods? Still worse yet, what if we lose our lives or we lose people close to us to this virus? So much feels uncertain.

So how do we navigate the mental health challenges of the early stages of the pandemic, the ones that are responsible for the palpable anxiety right now?

The first thing we can do is begin to divide the world and our choices in it into two categories—that which we can control and that which we cannot. We can't know or control how long this will go on for or how bad it will get. We can't control if other people hoard all the toilet paper. We can't control if the local or state government issues a shelter-in-place order that closes your workplace or leaves your kids at home. And let me be clear: all these things stink. No one likes them. But these disruptions are necessary for the safety of the community. In this fractious time, this is one point on which we can all try to agree.

The second category of things is that which we can control. The first part of this list are things that we can choose *not* to do. For those of us who can work from home, we can get done what we need to do and call it a day. We can release ourselves from the expectation that we're going to write that novel or finish those photo albums when we're stuck at home. It's okay just to get by right now. Much of our bandwidth is taken up by managing the situation and our anxiety. As tempting as it may be to pour that additional drink to manage the nerves, we can choose to pass that up too.

Of the things we *can* choose, probably the most important one is our *attitude*. As Viktor Frankl noted from his vantage in a concentration camp, everything can be taken from us except our freedom to choose our attitude about a given circumstance. It is in this choice that we begin to find the seeds of meaning.

We can still control when we go to bed and when we wake up. We have an opportunity to practice slowness and to turn our attention inward. We can choose to have a meditation practice and choose to cultivate our inner lives. We can mindfully wash our hands or wipe down our doorknobs. We can choose how much news we consume or how much we engage with others on social media. We can choose to reach out to supportive people who buoy our spirits and steer away from those who drag us down. We can choose to smile at people at the grocery store and wave to our neighbors. We can let the other guy go at the stop sign. We can be kind. We can savor the time spent with family. Beauty is medicine. Most of us, even if we're sheltered in place, are still permitted to go outside (just away from other people or crowds), and on these walks and bike rides, we can notice the color of the sky at sunset or the way that spring is announcing itself with a riot of flowers all around us.

Depression, Grief, and Sorrow

TS Elliot begins his epic poem "The Waste Land" with the line, "April is the cruelest month." And, indeed, April 2020 turned out to be just that. Our first responses, marked initially by denial and then anxiety-driven anger and bargaining, have, for some, now given way to depression—perhaps not clinical depression, but we certainly find ourselves in the grips of grief and sorrow. The breadth of this event has left no one untouched, but not all those who are touched have been impacted equally. This leads to a disorienting sense of separation and, at the same time, a singularity brought about by a unifying event.

The losses have taken many forms. The world has been stripped of its familiarity and its safety. We feel unable to control what comes next. There is a loss of the routine of going to work each day and the myriad of small interactions—saying hello to the person across the hall and the few minutes of banter before the staff meeting—that bring texture and pleasure to our days. The simple joys of social life—seeing a family member, meeting a friend for coffee, and exchanging a laugh and a hug—have been reduced to phone calls and boxes on a teleconference screen. But these losses pale when compared to those who have watched a loved one succumb to this illness, navigate the chaos of an overtaxed hospital, and die alone on a ventilator.

The feeling of loss is palpable right now even if we don't know anyone who has been sickened or died. We are suffering the loss of our ordinary lives, and we didn't even know how much we loved these lives and how much we were taking them for granted until they were gone. There is lassitude in the air, and there is deep sorrow. Meanwhile, spring announces itself with a riot of flowers and glorious cloudscapes.

My teacher Francis Weller has taught me that grief is an appropriate response to loss, but that losing the things that we love is not the only reason for grief. We are experiencing grief for other things too, including the things that we had hoped for, but did not get. There is also the grief of feeling alone and not being seen and witnessed by a supportive community. And there is also the ancestral grief that we carry and the collective grief of the world. All these places of grief are alive right now.

We do not grieve that which we do not care about. But sometimes it is only when the ordinary has been taken from us do we realize how much we loved our ordinary life before the loss. When it is gone, we wish we had praised it more, and we wish we could savor that which we once took for granted.

We Are Not in the Same Boat

Damian Barr

I heard that we are all in the same boat, but it's not like that. We are in the same storm, but not in the same boat. Your ship could be shipwrecked, and mine might not be or vice versa.

For some, quarantine is optimal—a moment of reflection, of reconnection, easy in flip-flops, with a cocktail or coffee. For others, this is a desperate financial and family crisis.

For some who live alone, they're facing endless loneliness. While for others it is peace, rest, and time with their mother, father, sons, and daughters.

With the $600 weekly increase in unemployment, some are bringing in more money to their households than when they were working. Others are working more hours for less money because of pay cuts or loss in sales.

Some families of four just received $3400 from the stimulus while other families of four saw $0.

Some were concerned about getting a certain candy for Easter while others were concerned if there would be enough bread, milk, and eggs for the weekend.

Some want to go back to work because they don't qualify for unemployment and are running out of money. Others want to kill those who break the quarantine.

Some are home, spending ten to 12 hours/day, helping their child with online schooling while others are spending two to three hours/day, educating their children on top of a ten- to 12-hour workday.

Some have experienced a near death because of the virus, some have already lost someone from it, and some are not sure if their loved ones are going to make it. Others don't believe this is a big deal.

Some have faith in God and expect miracles during 2020. Others say the worst is yet to come.

So, friends, we are not in the same boat. We are going through a time when our perceptions and needs are completely different.

Each of us will emerge, in our own way, from this storm. It is very important to see beyond what is seen at first glance—not just looking, but also actually seeing.

We are all on different ships during this storm, experiencing a very different journey.

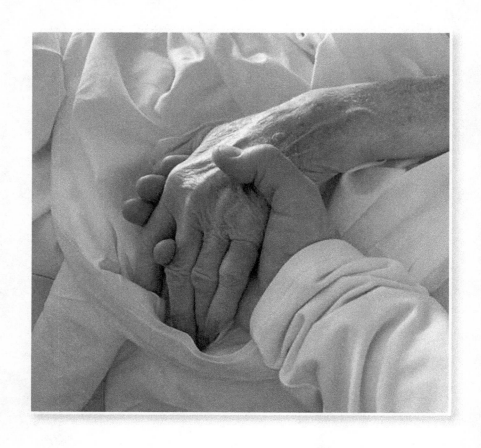

PL's Last Song

Gretchen Volk

I volunteered on a COVID unit at a public hospital in Brooklyn for a week in April of 2020. I am a general pediatrician in my real life and wasn't sure the State of New York would take me up on my offer to help during the coronavirus pandemic, but as the number of sick patients mounted and the curves of illness and death stretched ever upward, I got the call to go.

I understood that I would not be prepared for this, but I volunteer yearly at a clinic in Guatemala and know that I can handle adversity and uncertainty. My greatest fear was that I would arrive and find myself to be useless. That was certainly not the case. I was a doctor, a nurse, a social worker, a friend, and a substitute family member. I also understood that my gift of five days was a drop in the bucket compared to what my colleagues, permanently stationed in Brooklyn, had been and would continue to give, and so I brought cheer and Easter candy as well.

The list of things that surprised me was long and included both positives and negatives. The hotel gifted to me by the State of New York was in an unsafe neighborhood, and every inch of it smelled like marijuana. My Uber drivers hailed from Jamaica, Jordan, Haiti, and Ghana and shared home remedies, political perspectives, and blessings from their families. The hospital itself was both strange and familiar. While it had been decades since I had officially rounded on the wards with a medical team, it was easy enough to slip back into the familiar pattern of all hospital doctors—the call-and-response chorus from attending physician to intern to resident as we made morning rounds, chart rounds, and hypoxia rounds.

What completely took me by surprise was how I fell in love with my patients. I'm a kid person. I like to shoot the breeze with seven-year-olds, make goofy faces at babies, and pretend to eat toddlers' toes. And now here I was, surrounded by people in their sixties, seventies, and eighties who were fighting for their lives, and most horrifying of all, they were alone. I have never seen a hospital without visitors before, and as pesky as family members can be, I will tell you now that their role in patient care is invaluable. Countless times I walked into patients' rooms and found an oxygen mask fallen onto the floor or water too far away from a thirsty mouth.

PL was a 76-year-old lady with pulmonary fibrosis and eyes that sparkled. She had a lot to say as she huffed and puffed under the oxygen mask attached to her face. She said the kind of things other patients were too scared or too tired to admit: "Don't leave me" and "I'm afraid." This was hard to hear when you needed to keep moving on to the next patient in a 36-bed unit, so when I could, I would steal back to her bedside to talk. I learned that her grandmother was a Cherokee. Her grandfather was from an island. She grew up in North Carolina and missed its beautiful trees. Her children and grandchildren had a history of military service, and some were currently serving overseas while she fought her own battle against COVID-19 in Brooklyn. In later conversations, she told me she used to be a funeral director. How strange it was to watch her battling the possibility of death while at the same time she was so familiar with it professionally.

My father died this past fall while I was at an airport, trying desperately to get from New York to Los Angeles. I always thought I would be by his side when he took his last breath. How arrogant I was to think I could be the master of cancer's schedule—*pancreatic* cancer's schedule, no less. I absorbed the news of his death while on a shuttle between terminals A and D at Dulles. I sat alone, amid a crowd of people, reading the news from a text message on my phone. A young nun sat to my right, probably seven feet away from me, and I wondered if I should tell her. *Shouldn't someone else besides me know about this right now?* But as I said, she was young, and I wasn't sure she would be prepared for what was boiling inside me at that moment. I spared her this awkward conversation.

In Brooklyn my patients battled for their own lives, and unlike my father who did have loved ones with him, they were alone. On the last day of PL's life, she told me she had been trained as an opera singer. I asked her if she would sing to me. With ten liters of oxygen blasting into her face, she sang to me in French. I wish I could remember the song. Its melody, like its singer, now eludes me, but sing she did, and her wispy voice was unexpectedly beautiful. I turned her oxygen down a tiny bit, and we cheered together at the progress she was making that afternoon.

A few hours later, I peeked back in and was shocked at the change that had come over her. She was in frank respiratory distress, her mind focused only on breathing and the anxiety about not breathing. I cranked up her oxygen and stayed with her for a few minutes before running to get the rest of my team. We sat with her for an hour, initially providing reassurance, and then when that no longer seemed sufficient, we called for reinforcements from respiratory therapy.

We waited for an agonizing hour for the respiratory therapist to come. I held her hand and rubbed her head and reminded her to think about the forests of North Carolina. After PL finally switched to bi-pap, she got worse, and I realized that I was about to witness a futile and violent fight. The weapons of modern medicine were not enough to vanquish this awful virus from PL's already exhausted lungs, these same lungs that had sung for me in French just a few hours earlier.

I FaceTimed PL's family from my phone so they could see her struggle and asked their permission to change course. My goal was to give my friend peace and comfort. I couldn't beat this virus. All I could do was tell it that we weren't going to play by its rules anymore. Success for my friend would be defined by peace and nothing more than that. We gave her Dilaudid and switched her to a more comfortable oxygen mask. I held her hand until she was able to drift to sleep, and then I called her family again so they could see that she was at peace.

I felt guilty leaving the hospital that night. I wanted to stay with PL until her last moment, but I was due back on the unit in the morning, and I did not know how long she would live. I left her resting comfortably and in the care of two of the most compassionate residents I have had the privilege to know. She died about an hour before my next shift started. I will never forget PL—her sparkling eyes and beautiful voice and strong hands that squeezed mine back.

Likewise, I will never forget my week in Brooklyn and the lessons COVID-19 taught me. It was a week of death and life and cheering for those who got better and mourning for those who didn't.

And now I know that I am someone prone to falling in love with my fellow humans even if it means it will break my heart as well. I am a richer person for knowing PL, and I am honored that she shared some of her last moments with me even though I am now left with a lump in my throat when I remember that she could sing so beautifully mere hours before the virus took her away.

The Final Chapter

Teresa Schreiber Werth

Writing the final chapter
Of your life, the time has come.
Pages gilt with the gold of memories
Delicious, happy, brilliant moments
Telling the story of you,
Charting the trajectory of your
Personal trail of stardust.
These final pages
Difficult, painful,
Not the ending you envisioned.
Caught in the quicksand of the virus
Watching the clock whose greedy hands
Reach out to pull you in.
Release your fear of leaving
To the fog of the unknown.
Close your weary eyes, drink in the stillness
Step off into a brand-new life, new bones.
Knowing we are left with
The essence of you
Everywhere, always.

Incredible Courage

Virginia Cross

God loves each of us as if there
were only one of us.
—Saint Augustine

Each evening on the news, we hear accounts of courage, stories of medical staff in hospitals: doctors, nurses, support persons, transport people, and first responders, and stories about police and firefighters, volunteers, and many others caring for those who have been infected with COVID-19. They all show incredible courage each hour of each day, and we are grateful. We need to thank them profusely, with our words and with our overflowing hearts.

But what about *you*? You were the one at the bedside of your family member or friend. You saw them getting worse from the virus. You knew that their only chance of survival was to have them go into the hospital where they could be cared for and be given more than you could provide. It took incredible courage for you to say goodbye to them when the ambulance arrived and you were told that you could not go with them.

Or, perhaps, you took your family member or friend to a medical facility and were told you could not go in with them. The door closed, and you had to say goodbye with the closed door between you. That took incredible courage. Now you are grieving the loss of your family member or friend. You have incredible courage to keep on going each day.

In my service as a hospital chaplain at the University of Rochester Medical Center in Rochester, New York, I would visit patients in their rooms. One day on the unit, I came to two rooms side by side. In one room, there was a person who was dying, surrounded by eight loved ones who were singing and praying for them. It was beautiful to see. In the room next to that was a lone man also dying who had no one praying for him or singing to him. As I stayed with him and prayed for him, I wondered about God.

Does God quantify prayer? Does God reason, "This person has a lot of people praying for them, so they are much more valuable than this other person who has only one person praying for them"? My faith informed my decision that the *number* of people praying for someone is not a factor in how much God loves them and cares for them. I felt God's presence as I sat and prayed with a dying man that day. And I saw God's presence in the room next door.

If your loved one died without you being there—in a hospital room, ambulance, nursing home, or at home—it took incredible courage on your part to let them go. It took incredible courage on their part to face death without you. Yet God was with both of you. Neither of you was alone—incredible courage.

Courage is front and center on the world stage of this pandemic. In ways, large and small, we see it every minute of every day—incredible courage.

This Spring Will Be Remembered

Emily Kedar

That spring
When all we could hear
Was birdsong
When we learned to sprout seed
Bake bread, mold candles

Wait

When the sham
Of the busy life
Broke open and fell
Round our ankles

When each of us
On our own
Chose to open
Our doors
To place our bare feet
On the wet March earth

And stopped moving around
So much.

When we noticed finally
Which tree the crows
Have been nesting in
These last long years,
And how they torment
The robins

When we learned to speak crow,
Treebud, rainfall,
When we remembered how
To be silent and found
The spacious side of stillness

Waiting

When we learned
That the small daily dances:
Going out and coming home,
Matter

And can moor strangers
Back to safety,
Somehow, miraculously.

That spring we braved to slow,
Shrugged the voice
That's been insisting
We won't ever be enough.

That spring we learned
That each touched surface
Held us
Long after we were gone

That we were already
Earthbody
Already arriving
Already bridging worlds.

Essential Workers without Benefits

Maria Delgado Sutton

In a world of COVID-19, I am blessed—yes, blessed—to realize that I *understand* what is going on with this pandemic that has taken over the world.

Every morning, I quietly prepare myself a cup of green tea before turning on the television or my computer to listen to *the facts*...facts that I now only trust from scientists, doctors, and nurses. Knowledge is the key to understanding what I can do to protect myself and everyone I encounter.

As a nurse, my hand has always been extended to those in need. Since I am at the forefront of this pandemic, I know that I must be informed of the ever-changing protocols and options available for those I serve.

Late last week, I received a telephone call from a friend of mine. Her name is Antonia, and she is in a panic. She explains that she was fired from work and does not understand why. Antonia is a diabetic with no health insurance. She lives paycheck to paycheck to pay for her diabetic supplies. What little she has left she uses to pay for groceries and send to her mother in Mexico. Antonia is an undocumented migrant farmworker. She wakes every morning at five and heads to the packing plant to pack vegetables or fruits or to the fields to plant. Everything she touches at work is sent out to markets all over our region.

I ask her more questions, and through her tears and muffled voice, I begin to realize that Antonia, though aware of COVID-19, does not understand the gravity of this pandemic. Through conversations with her coworkers (there are six in total), she knows that *la corona* is a virus, like the flu, but she has no idea how contagious or lethal it is. I hear desperation in her voice.

A normal routine for her consists of working six days a week, sunup till sundown. A television, newspaper, or computer is nonexistent in her world. They are not items of necessity. She lives alone in a run-down one-bedroom cement-block house, located in a strip of five houses just like hers. Antonia has always lived in a secluded area. Trust me, she is invisible. You would never find her. Her community has always been at risk and lives mostly in the shadows. Antonia has been afraid and invisible since the first day she arrived in the United States five years ago, seeking a better life for herself.

After a few more questions, I convince her to send a text to her employer in English, which I help her compose, asking why she was let go. Luckily, he responds immediately, "You're not fired. I gave you the next two weeks off because of the virus. I know that you are a diabetic, and you seemed a little sick. I will still pay you for the two weeks off. Take care of yourself, and stay quarantined. I am sorry if I didn't explain it right."

I immediately wonder if he is supplying his employees with masks, gloves, sanitizers, and up-to-date information. Do they have what they need to properly clean their homes? What is he doing to protect his farm?

Antonia is relieved. No, she is elated! She is even laughing, suddenly understanding why there are such long lines at Walmart, why some people are wearing masks, and why some have gloves on. I quickly tell Antonia about some of the important resources that are out there for her. She can get food through Foodlink. Other dry goods are available at her community food cupboard. Several area churches are offering prepared meals. I supply her with fact sheets in Spanish on COVID-19. I give her the number of the COVID National Support Center. I also explain that she will not qualify for the stimulus check that is being distributed to most Americans. She does not qualify for any government support, health care, or unemployment even though she is an essential employee as a farmworker.

I advise her to call her doctor about her cough. We review her medications. Does she have enough to last her until her next paycheck? How long will her insulin last? Does she have enough groceries? (I wish I were there to give her an extra mask I know I have in my bag.) Antonia is crying. Now that she understands the reality of her situation, she is afraid.

I know exactly what questions are racing through her mind: Should I tell my employer if I get any symptoms? What will happen if I get sick with the virus? How will I pay for the ambulance to take me to the hospital? How will I pay for that hospital bill? Will my employer let me work again if he finds out that I have COVID-19?

Antonia also worries about her family far away in Mexico. Has COVID-19 reached there? She is worried about her two children, one in Connecticut and one still in Mexico. Are they safe from this disease? And who is checking on her mother who is 88 years old?

While Antonia is now up to speed on the pandemic, I apologize for not checking in on her sooner. My work as a nurse, a term

67

that now qualifies me as an essential employee, has been consumed with taking care of others. My shifts have doubled since the virus has reared its ugly head. All my patients are in the high-risk group. Not only is my own health risk heightened, but also that of my family. Life has always been a high-stakes game, but it is now more than ever.

As we say goodbye, I wonder how many Antonias are out there. How many of them don't understand what is happening in the world around them or have the resources to deal with it and be safe?

I know today will be a busier day than usual. I'll be calling all my farmworker families.

Discovering Hope in Desperate Times

James Sutton

Being homeless sucks. As with most subpopulations in America, you can't generalize who a typical homeless person is. Everything in life is on a spectrum. On one end of the spectrum, there are normal, hardworking people who just fell upon hard times. They lost their job or were victims of abuse or fell into an addiction or just made some bad life decisions that led to nowhere to live. Many on that end of the spectrum aren't truly homeless in the way you would think. They often are doubling up—that is, they are living in the basement of someone else's house, sleeping on a couch. Then there is the homeless person living in a shelter with no money, car, food, family, or life. They may be the street dwellers who stand on corners, begging for change, and curl up behind a building downtown at night to sleep. Regardless of where a person falls on the homeless spectrum, the best way to describe their situation is that it sucks.

How do you take a terrible situation like that and make it worse? Add a pandemic!

Frank was homeless. It was sort of his fault and sort of not his fault. He grew up in a broken family with an alcoholic father and was raised by a single mother. He dropped out of high school and fell into the wrong crowd. By his midtwenties he was working under the table, doing construction and living in a small apartment downtown. He had some PTSD and mental health issues and saw a local therapist periodically for medications and therapy. Life wasn't great, but he managed to make it from day to day. Frank was a tall, skinny redhead with an infectious smile who laughed at everything. He was kind and gentle, and people described him as a thinker. People liked to hang out with him, but if he drank too much, his mood got dark, and his demons sometimes emerged. One day his anger got the best of him, and he got into a fight at work and was told to not come back. Later that night, he used heroin for the first time and got into a silly brawl at a corner store where he was arrested. Having no attorney, he ended up going to prison for a year over the altercation. When he got out, he was intent on turning his life around. He got into a halfway house, got connected with a mental health provider, started a job-training program, and could see light at the end of the tunnel. His ear-to-ear smile had returned. Then the pandemic hit.

The first week of the new stay-at-home orders saw the halfway house staff cut by two-thirds. Rules were loosened, and some of the residents were able to sneak in drugs. Frank resisted and stayed to himself. His job-training program shut down because of the virus, and his supply of medications for PTSD was running out. His scheduled appointment with a social worker, in order to keep his insurance and benefits active, was canceled and postponed for a few weeks. He used the pay phone in the lobby to call his mental health provider for refills, but when he got to the pharmacy, his Medicaid had been deactivated, and he couldn't get the meds. Frank hung in there. He continued to stay to himself and kept saying, "Things will eventually get better." His smile was still there, but not as wide as before. He had been without his meds for about a week.

On Saturday night he got into an argument with another resident who was teasing him about not using. He exploded, and the lone staff member at the house called the cops. "This is BS!" he shouted at the cops. With that, he was kicked out of the house and taken to the House of Mercy homeless shelter. That was when things went from bad to worse.

With minimal staff and a constant flow of transient guests, the shelter experience had changed because of the pandemic. Everyone wore masks 24-7. No contact was allowed among the residents. Food was shipped in, and residents went through the line six feet apart and ate alone.

People in the suburbs spent their shelter-in-place at home, masks off, watching TV and talking with family. Frank spent four weeks isolated from all human contact, alone. That smile was now completely gone, and the brightness in his eyes had dulled. The light at the end of his tunnel was completely extinguished.

I saw Frank for a medical visit, and his chief complaint was, "I have a problem." Yes, he needed some medicine. Yes, he needed a social worker to help him get back on track. Yes, he needed to reengage with his job training. These were all givens, but it was difficult to deduce what exactly *the real problem* was. After 45 minutes of conversation it became clear that *the real problem* was that he had lost hope. The pandemic hit just when he was gaining hope for a new life.

We see news reports of people losing lives from COVID-19, but often forget how it can destroy lives without actually causing a death. Frank's life was destroyed by the virus. It wasn't the cough and fever. It was a month of isolation while watching all his plans and progress fall apart.

It has now been about a month since I started seeing Frank. He is back on his medications and seeing a therapist weekly (by phone). A social worker was able to reactivate his Medicaid and benefits and get him back into a transitional living environment. His job-training program is opening back up in a couple of weeks, but will be virtual. A local nonprofit gave him an iPad so he could attend. I saw him yesterday, and the smile was back, but his eyes still weren't quite as bright. A sliver of hope seemed to have taken hold inside of him again.

It has been said that a person needs just three things to be truly happy in this world: someone to love, something to do, and something to hope for. The virus robbed Frank of all three.

I am sure this pandemic will pass. Most things do. And as we move back out into the world and think about ways we can help other people, remember Frank. Visiting a homeless shelter or working a soup line aren't just about helping people. It is about giving hope. Hope can be a powerful force. Maybe there's no actual magic in it, but when you have hope, it is like a light within you...almost like magic.

Musings on Moving (in Corona Times)

Mara Ahmed

April 9, 2020

Earlier in January, I had hired a local business to move us from Rochester to Long Island on April 8. Then COVID-19 hit, and our movers backed out of driving to New York City, right in the eye of the pandemic. The owner was a small businessman with young children. He said he didn't want to take chances. I understood.

So the new movers came by and loaded our trucks yesterday. Yes, we ended up renting two trucks instead of one—my bounteous artwork, packed in some 20 to 30 large boxes, was partly to blame.

This morning we traveled as a caravan—my husband driving a 26-foot truck, my son managing a 20-foot truck, my daughter driving our sedan, and yours truly forging ahead in an SUV. All I can say is, it's good to have grown-up kids.

Navigation was easy all the way—empty highways, not more than two or three cars in service areas, a few people scurrying around, wearing masks, no toll tickets, and no delays on approaching New York City. The George Washington Bridge seemed haunted. There were just two cars in front of me. In my 27 years of living around and traveling frequently to New York, I'd never seen anything like it. It felt disturbingly quiet, unnatural, and somber. Throughout the trip signs on highways urged people to stay at home, limit travel, and stop the spread, #flattenthecurve.

My brother called to find out how we were doing. The car picked up his phone call. He told me his ex-neighbor in New Jersey, the guy they lived next to for a whole decade and who saw his kids grow up, just died of coronavirus. He had an allergic reaction to something, went to the ER, got infected, and died within a few days—in his early fifties. I am not one to panic, but this piece of news shook me.

So between these misgivings (could we have delayed the closing on our house?); the thrill of living next to a city I love; the waves of emotion as I realized I was gradually moving away from the people I love; the profusion of texts, e-mails, and phone calls from family and friends, all holding me warmly in their prayers and good wishes; the bone-tiredness from packing up a commodious house filled with 17 years of life and film and art making; and finally, the news that Bernie Sanders had just ended his presidential run, I couldn't quite focus on any one feeling.

Yet there was a connection—a complete sense of disconnection: being uprooted with milestones and memories packed precariously in cardboard boxes, the fear of losing people we love, the undignified randomness of loss, the arbitrariness of what we mark as ours in time and space, the irrationality of viruses and politics, the fragility of life and human-made systems, and the strength of love and relationships that bind us to a center—some multifaceted, metaphysical core that saves us from disintegrating into meaningless fragments.

We are home, in this new home. It's a gorgeous apartment—small, but perhaps, that's all we need for our small family. The kids are here. Everyone is asleep. Good night, fam, and please stay safe.

The New Coronavirus Rules

Adam Lazarus

This Coronavirus has struck quite a nerve.
Worldwide we're all trying to flatten the curve.

I'm following the rules and doing my part.
To stay safe and healthy, while staying apart.

I'm doing the things to fight COVID-19.
Like washing my hands and a self-quarantine.

I'm hand sanitizing. Ain't touching my face.
Been staying at home. I'm sheltered in place.

I'm socially distanced—staying 6 feet away.
Not hoarding toilet paper or cleaning spray.

But the precautions I'm taking are just not enough.
I think I need new rules, more stringent and tough.

Since March was so awful and today's April Fools,
I've written a new set of pandemic rules!

Stay 6 feet away? I'm making it 20.
No hugs. No high fives. A head nod is plenty.

If anyone sneezes near me—they get smacked.
If they cough? For that—they get fully attacked!

You're handwashing three times a day? Make it ten.
You just washed your hands? Then go wash 'em again!

Using hand sanitizer liberally won't do.
Douse yourself in it. Then drink that stuff too.

Forget surgical masks, I want full Hazmat suits!
In public. At home. And for all car commutes.

Feel sick? Stay at home. Forever! Stay there.
Feeling better? Don't care. Never go anywhere.

Hoard toilet paper? You're on a "checkup" list,
Performed by a shaky blind Proctologist.

Need groceries or want supplies from the store?
Unless it's essential, you get nothing. No more!

Seek medical attention if you're feeling ill.
And if your test comes back positive? Move to Brazil.

If you own a house, then you must build a dome.
A protective germ bubble surrounding your home.

And last but not least, when everything's better,
Each doctor and nurse gets a long thank you letter.

My rules sound extreme. And they may seem unfair.
But this virus is nasty. So, I really don't care.

I hope you enjoyed my new tongue-and-cheek rules.
Stay healthy. Stay humorous. And enjoy April Fools!

Finding Heart

Cecile Carson

When incomprehensible and overwhelming events and losses bring us to our knees, when we feel the breakup of our ordered lives, and when we can't make sense of things and experience heartbreak and unfairness, that's the time when our regular minds are jettisoned, and we are forced to move into our hearts. Deep grief fills us, and we find that we are in a dark forest with no clear path. And we recognize there is no way around it and no way back to the way things were. In that free fall, we know our lives will never be the same.

If we are lucky, in that profound disruption, we begin to let go of figuring it all out and, instead, drop into the vast realm of the heart—a sacred place of Mystery, of profound relatedness to those we love beyond physical words and touch. That place has no closed doors.

Only the heart can make it right. Only the heart knows the way, knows the things that need to be said, and teaches us to honor the mystery of not knowing the why of this loss in this way.

We must do what the Ancient Ones did when their loved ones were taken by disease or by a predator animal or fell to their deaths. They went to their knees, they keened, they used ritual to invoke the Larger Order of Things for help and guidance, and they were held by their tribe in their grief. We must move beyond what our Western culture teaches about separateness and aloneness. We are all in this together.

The heart space shows us the way to honorable grief, the grief beyond our ego, beyond blaming or judging. Honorable grief lets us say through our hearts the words left unsaid. Through the heart, we can send the energy of our love to bring comfort, reassurance, and release to our loved ones from their suffering and chaos. We can send the heart's light we all carry to guide us and our loved ones on the separate paths ahead of us. And through the heart we can allow ourselves to receive absolution for not being able to be with them and for all the times we forgot to say "I love you" and "I forgive you." We can begin to move on.

Tragedy breaks us open from our fixed forms and understandings to make us realize that we are not separate and alone. All of life has its own energy, its own spirit, and its own way through the world. No one would voluntarily choose tragedy, but over and over again we realize the hidden messages and meanings that can emerge as we move through the dark forest. In our heart's vast realm of relatedness to all things, we realize there is a way into a new ordering of our world and that the heart can lead the way, beyond the physical world, where we are not separate or cut off.

There are simple acts that can help us offer honorable grief to ourselves and others. They connect our bodies to our heart space to help move us through the darkness:

1. Asking for help—prayer helps us lean into the direction our heart is pointing us as we speak our deep truth about our loss.

2. Naming and sharing the grief—both writing down our thoughts to express them on paper (journaling) and sharing our feelings with others to begin to move the grief through us.

3. Simple rituals of releasing—asking the elements of this world to take our grief to help us unburden: (a) lying face-down on the Earth, placing our heart against her, and asking her to take our pain, transform it, and give it back to the world as pure energy; (b) writing the words of grief on a piece of paper and asking Fire to burn and release the pain of the words; and (c) asking Air to lift up a balloon we've filled with the breath of our grief to let the vastness of the sky soften and dilute it.

4. Releasing our loved one from our attachment to them in this life—saying what has been left unsaid and then sending out our love and light to them for a safe journey Home. Their soul needs our help in moving on.

5. Singing—song lets us shape and give voice to the grief, clearing and freeing the difficult feelings caught in our bodies: songs of lament, songs of remembrance, and special songs that keep us connected to our loved ones through time.

6. Being open to receive messages from our loved one from the sacred place of Mystery—noticing those small, but spacious moments when you feel a direct connection to them: when a bird they loved comes to your window; when in a difficult moment you're having, you hear a particular song of theirs on the radio; or when in a twilight state before

sleep, you feel a gentle touch on your cheek when no one is physically there.

7. Tending to ourselves through setting limits and offering a blessing—being very careful about the amount of news you allow yourself and taking in just enough to be informed without being overwhelmed and retraumatized by seeing the same terrible event over and over again. If you change from TV reports to newspaper or e-news, you can run your hand over the report and ask for a blessing from Source or God for those involved in the news.

There is no right or wrong way through grief if you let your heart guide you. Each person's grief is as unique as they are. Be gentle with yourself. Make small steps. And remember, you are never alone.

Find Your Peace in the Pandemic

Jillian Harrison-Jones

On February 23, 2020, Ahmaud Arbery of Brunswick, Georgia, was shot and killed while jogging by two white American males who dared to accuse him of burglarizing their neighborhood. He was unarmed. Breonna Taylor, an EMT from Louisville, Kentucky, was fatally shot in her home on March 13 by police who entered the wrong home in pursuit of an alleged drug bust. She was unarmed. We are faced with a devastating reality: COVID-19 and the nationwide stay-at-home order have not stopped the injustices toward Black Americans from happening. On one hand, COVID-19 disproportionately attacks and kills Black Americans at alarming rates because of preexisting conditions such as hypertension, diabetes, asthma, cancer, obesity, and hypercholesterolemia; on the other hand, Black Americans are still being shot and killed in cold blood by police and self-acclaimed neighborhood watchmen who happen to be white. Black Americans are running out of hands.

Black Americans are running out of hands, yet we continue to fight and rally. Black Americans are running out of hands, yet we continue to pray. Black Americans are running out of hands, yet we continue to serve, build, and educate tomorrow's leaders. Black Americans are running out of hands, yet we continue to write books and create music and art. Historically, Black Americans have been the most resilient of American communities. Surviving 400 years of slavery, Jim Crow, lynching (past and present-day), police brutality, and so much more, we could all stand to learn from the resilience of Black Americans.

What can the world stand to learn about Black Americans and the will we possess to stand up and fight another day? The Black community is just that: a community. Imagine living in a world where people look just like you, where, at every turn, you can see yourself in someone else, and instead of being threatened by this image, you celebrate and uplift this image. To talk about the amount of Black-on-Black crime is shortsighted and narrow-minded; there is more unity in the Black community than there is not. From artistic spaces (in person or virtual) to churches and faith communities, from fraternities and sororities to CEOs and entrepreneurs, Black America has stood and continues to stand strong in its will to live and thrive. Black Americans find solace in philanthropic projects, social engagement, creativity through the arts and music, and so much more; but most importantly, Black Americans find solace in Divine Fellowship.

Black churches have played a pivotal role in the mental, physical, and emotional survival and well-being of Black Americans during this pandemic, not solely on the basis of preaching the Gospel and singing of songs via Facebook Live, but also through the proactive and inventive nature of providing opportunities for betterment in practical ways. Cases in point are Reverend Dr. Winterbourne Harrison-Jones and the Witherspoon Presbyterian Church of Indianapolis, Indiana (a predominantly Black congregation). The leadership and creativity of Pastor Harrison-Jones and the Witherspoon staff have led to the most tangible of virtual interaction opportunities to engage

Indianapolis and the nation as Pastor Harrison-Jones reminds the community daily that "the doors of the true church are never closed."

Witherspoon's history has always been rooted deeply in the arts and music, where the musical culture of the church ranges from jazz to gospel to western classical traditions and so much more. Witherspoon has continued in its weekly "Sweet Hour of Prayer" each Friday at noon, featuring an hour-long service of live music and a brief homily. Witherspoon has also continued its Sacred Arts Concert Series virtually, which has featured solo recitals from world-renowned artists such as Dr. Tedrin Lindsay, Mr. Rob Dixon, and Mr. Myron Williams. Other opportunities for the arts include the church's youth ministry. Pastor Josiah McCruiston has implemented a project entitled the "Book Nook," which features stories from the Rufus and Susie Meyer's Children's Book Collection, books by African American authors housed at Witherspoon. This opportunity offers the youth of Witherspoon to engage virtually every week with a book that they can relate to: stories in which they can see themselves.

The initiatives of Pastors Harrison-Jones and McCruiston keep the doors of Witherspoon "open" and put this faith community at the forefront of demonstrating what church vitality looks like. These are opportunities that continue to give our community *hope* through this pandemic.

Similarly, an arts organization in Cincinnati has also found ways to regularly engage its community, for the arts have played a crucial role in the emotional and mental health of audiences and performers alike. As the music director of MUSE, Cincinnati's Women's Choir, I can attest that this pandemic has brought this community of artists and activists together, arguably closer than any in-person activity could do. MUSE is an organization that advocates for social justice and equality for communities that are underrepresented and overlooked, and we advocate through music and community collaborations.

MUSE has been innovative in our approach toward artistic expression and performance. We work internally to keep our members artistically stimulated while finding new ways to engage and expand our community and support base. Since the social-distancing order was issued in March 2020, MUSE has continued to rehearse virtually via Zoom every Monday evening. While the objective is to offer a schedule that is reminiscent of a normal season, we meet and engage through a myriad of things, including full-choir rehearsals, sectionals, social activities, and workshops. MUSE is determined to keep the arts alive. Keeping our organization engaged through weekly and, sometimes, daily activities has been vital for the mental and emotional well-being of our membership. From large and small group activities and weekly accountability groups, we have created a level of intimacy and safety within our community.

These are the things that have kept me at peace daily. These are the things that give us all hope and make us resilient.

www.musechoir.org
MUSE Virtual Choir Project: Sisters You Keep Me Fighting
https://youtu.be/8yJ1Rslef0c

www.wpcindy.org
Got Something to Say–Actors Ink Production
https://www.facebook.com/wpcindy2/videos/286738664020679

What Are You Creating Now?

Teresa Schreiber Werth

I recently read an article by Carolyn Edlund of *Artsy Shark* about artists and the pandemic. The subtitle of the piece was, "No one is untouched by the dramatic changes caused by the COVID-19 pandemic. How are artists coping, and what are they doing?"

She recently asked artists, "How have your plans changed? What are you doing now?" and received hundreds of responses from around the world. The vast majority of artists were steadfastly positive, saying that they were doing the following:

- Making art
- Baking bread
- Resting and healing
- Entering online art competitions
- Practicing yoga
- Updating their art websites
- Publishing free art courses on YouTube
- Taking free art courses on YouTube
- Sending inspirational newsletters
- Praying
- Sewing masks for hospital workers

- Growing produce for food banks
- Writing a book
- Working on commissions
- Playing with toddlers
- Caring for the elderly
- Mentoring others
- Participating in collaborative online art projects
- Cleaning and reorganizing their studios
- Learning better business skills
- Keeping a regular studio schedule
- Creating coloring pages for others to download
- Making art videos for kids
- Participating in virtual art walks
- Donating a portion of their sales to support artists and others in need
- Transitioning their in-person art classes to online teaching
- Mastering YouTube and Facebook Live
- Taking long, hot baths
- Recording podcasts
- Encouraging and supporting others
- Designing home-school art lesson plans
- Going with the flow
- Committing random acts of kindness

It is an exhilarating list! When people are deprived of their livelihood or their passion (or both), it's easy to fall into a slump, to brood, or to feel as if the air has been sucked out of you. I am heartened by the list Ms. Edlund has shared.

My guess is that the list is, at least, somewhat true across the art world, not applicable to just visual artists. Musical performances and live theaters have stopped. Choir rehearsals and orchestras have gone silent. Art galleries and art shows have disappeared. The making of all types of art is suffering and searching for new ways to exist.

Our 17-year-old grandson (deprived of a normal high-school graduation by the pandemic) recently shared his observation that "there are winners and losers in everything, and this pandemic is no exception." The way those two piles play out may not make us happy or feel fair, but it is true. Some artists (and other people) are finding ways to make lemonade out of the lemons with which we've been showered! Others, despite their best efforts, are not faring so well.

In a recent conversation with international stained-glass artist Peter McGrain about how his work is going, he told me, "I can certainly say that making art, for me, has always been a fantastic coping skill, on a personal level, for providing an escape from boredom, isolation, fear, or anxiety in the same way that playing music or writing would."

Looking at Edlund's list, almost every item ends in -*ing*, indicating activity: making, baking, resting, healing, practicing, updating, and publishing—on and on it goes. You get the distinct feeling that these are not people who are *stuck*. In fact, they seem like some of the most *unstuck people* I have heard about in the past few months!

McGrain adds, "Creating stuff helps avoid the worrisome feeling that your head is about to explode from overload, whether there is a pandemic, political or social crisis, family crisis, or any of the rest of the psychological challenges of dealing with daily life. I guess that's why so many of us find therapeutic comfort when we immerse ourselves in our creative endeavors."

So, perhaps, as our grandson suggests, there may even be some artistic winners that emerge from this time of isolation, this seismic shift in our daily lives.

"On the other hand," says McGrain, "built-up feelings of joy and celebration are always best served when channeled into a fine, creative project. And, of course, apart from these self-indulgent reasons for creating, *sharing* these efforts, with a hope to inspire others, hopefully puts us all one step closer to achieving grace."

The Golden Hour

Gordon Webster

How precious life is! How can we sustain that conviction in April 2020 and beyond?

Just today the data shows 926,465 Americans have been infected with the coronavirus, or COVID-19, and of that number 47,590 have died. Today, April 25, the source of those numbers is the *New York Times*. What will the numbers be next week? Next month?

The news about New York's 5,200 nursing homes and other long-term care facilities is that today over 63,000 residents and staff are infected, and 10,500 have died. As chaplain of Rochester Presbyterian Home, located in the city's 19th ward, I thank God and the home's leadership team that none of the residents have been infected. Not one among the staff has been infected. But the data can change, and the data can cause fear.

The COVID-19 pandemic, an epidemic across the entire earth, threatens both our health and our economics. It has already over-whelmed our hospitals, our care centers, our health professionals, and our essential workers, especially in New York City. Like the national economy, as evidenced in the stock market's volatility, the headline of April 21, 2020, declares, "New York State's unemployment sys-tem 'collapsed' following a surge in jobless claims." As of mid-April, across the United States, "at least 22 million Americans have filed for unemployment insurance in four weeks, wiping out all the job gains since the Great Recession (2008–09)."

These figures, facts, and fears challenge our hopes for our future! Our hearts ache for all who are seriously affected. We wonder whether the world we lived in before this pandemic will ever return. Or could this be a golden opportunity for a reset—a time when we could all make better choices about how to live together and care for our planet and one another?

That is where the phenomenon of the golden hour may be able to ease our minds. John Dickerson of CBS News closed *60 Minutes* on April 19 by saying, "We need to pay attention to the golden hour. Keep it ever before us."

Even as I write these words on Saturday, April 25, the sun is angling toward its setting, its light increasingly gold. One hour before the sun sets is known to photographers as the golden hour. We experience it as beautiful rays through our dining room, kitchen, and laundry room windows, gently bathing our living spaces with warming, yet dying, light. Ever closer to setting, the sunlight embraces our rooms, that which furnishes them, the tables at which we sit, and the couch and chairs in which we settle. Then the blue of cloudless day gives way to the goldening of our yard's greenery so that the home in which we are advised to stay to save our lives and the lives of our neighbors—with whom we are social distancing—becomes the entrancing memory of our lives, one day at a time. Beauty overcomes the commonplace, and we begin again to learn that the *length* of our days is always enhanced by the blessed memorable *among* our days.

I cherish even more the light of late afternoon, a time when my grandmother suggested that I, a five-year-old, should rest awhile.

The light through her windows was from the golden hour of that day's ending.

The golden hour is also that hour following a wound to the human body. If a person is wounded, doctors know that their care of the wound is most successful if it is treated within 60 minutes of its infliction. Their success decreases every hour afterward that the patient spends waiting for ministrations to the wound to begin.

COVID-19 is a wound to our bodies. But before you or I, if we are infected, can begin treatment, we need to be seen by a medical professional. If the emergency room is overcrowded, if the intensive care unit (ICU) is overwhelmed, the golden hour is in danger of being reduced—not to mention the fact that our hope begins to diminish.

The third meaning of the golden hour is that hour just before the rising sun—the dawn of the day, the dawn of life! Let the life of children dawn! I want all three of my granddaughters to experience the joy of dawn's golden hour. Today they are ten, eight, and six-months old. May they be blessed with many healthy decades, leading them each to find their beloved—their gazelle or young stag—so each may approach the dawn of their time for the blessings of love. Which of their dawns will be the most blessed and memorable ones for them? Will their grandmothers and grandfathers participate in their dawning days? All are unknown tomorrows.

Recently, Gov. Cuomo announced that the data indicates that the peak of coronavirus infections in our state has passed—fewer and fewer people in New York are being infected. Fewer and fewer people are dying. Hospitals and intensive care units are no longer being overwhelmed. But the threat is not over. Even though we truly need to reopen our businesses—small and large—we are still not ready to go back to business as usual. If we reopen too soon, the very social distancing and staying home that prevent the spread of COVID-19 will no longer stand in the way of new cases. New infections will rise.

So as April gives way to May, let us pay attention to what has worked until infections come to a standstill. Let the golden hour preceding the sunrise each day give hope to more and more people—to recover from the coronavirus that put them in the hospital and to prevent infections from recurring.

Then as the threat diminishes to freedom from infection for whole populations in countries and states, we can turn to rebuilding our lives, community by community and reopened business by reopened economy.

In the days of recovery, we will thank God for the coming dawn of health and prosperity and keep the golden hour ever before us as the sunset gentles us into the evening.[1]

---

[1] As of mid-February, Gordon Webster has been hospitalized with COVID. He is stable, on a ventilator and progressing toward recovery.

Sharing Sacred Space

Gloria Osborne

For most of us, honoring our loved ones at the time of death is one of the most sacred obligations we have. Although it is not always possible to be at their side when they die, sometimes we can be there in other ways. And, certainly, we can continue to share our thoughts and feelings with them through prayer or simple intention. Prayer and meditation have become parts of many of our lives—creating change and healing wounds. So let's explore some ways of sustaining and supporting ourselves—many of us who may be alone and isolated during this time of widespread grief and suffering.

Perhaps, we can begin by creating a sacred time and place each day to nurture ourselves while sending prayers and thoughts to our beloved ones. I like to begin by grounding or centering myself so that I feel totally present and connected to the world around me. This could be finding a comfortable spot that holds special memories, either indoors or outdoors, and imagining loved ones there with you. Using all your senses to connect with the smells, sights, sounds, and feels of your environment, create a space for the memory of your loved one(s) as well. Remember what it was like to share a pleasant experience together, and select a poem, special reading, song, or other activity you can share in this moment as if your loved one were present. Remember that each thought, prayer, or intention is a form of energy that carries its meaning through time and space.

Both science and religion acknowledge this phenomenon— one as quantum physics and the other as spiritual connection. Truly, none of us are ever alone in this universe. Now more than ever it is important to remember all the ways we are connected. Although we cannot see or hear one another, we can recall one another's presence and cling to that memory. Having an object that belonged to him or her can bring comfort—a photograph, a piece of clothing, or a book—anything that helps to gather the spirit of that person closer. Depending on the circumstances, we might be asking for a safe recovery or a peaceful death. In either case we can talk to our loved one as if we were with them, letting them know what they mean to us and what we will always remember—favorite foods, vacations, private or family moments—whatever you feel your loved one would want to hear. For some, writing a letter or drawing pictures or keeping a journal of what is taking place during this separation can be helpful.

Remembering to care for yourself and your family is equally important. If you have close friends or family, they may be able to bring prepared food or assist with updates to other friends or family members. If you are alone, creating a phone tree might be easier so you can limit your time on the phone. Carve out some time for a hot bath or shower, and remember to breathe and relax, perhaps to some soothing background music. If you are a golfer, maybe just practice your golf swing. Bounce a ball, sing or play a musical instrument or drum, or practice yoga or tai chi, whatever soothes and relaxes you and helps to restore your body's natural balance.

Keep things simple. Now is not the time to start a new diet or tackle a difficult project. Allow yourself to feel compassion for yourself as well as your loved one by holding your hand over your heart and feeling the unconditional and unlimited love that resides there. Be gentle with yourself.

You Are Essential

Maria Delgado Sutton

When it comes to your loved ones in a nursing home or adult-care facility, never let anyone tell you, "You are not essential." This is my very strong opinion based on my personal and professional experience.

My parents recently passed away 42 days apart. They were my everything. God blessed me with an incredibly supportive family at home and siblings who understood the need for me to walk away from my nursing career in order to take care of my parents during the last three years of their life.

I have always loved working with the elderly. That is my niche in life—my calling. I have no doubt it is rooted in the many times my mom, a nursing assistant, took me and my sister to work with her. Back then, we would sit quietly in her patients' private homes and watch Mom fuss over her patients. She took such pride in caring for them. Dancing and singing around the room and seeing them smile made her beam with delight. She lovingly bathed them while whispering words of love, slathering them with perfumed lotion, and making sure each hair was in place. Their clothing had to be impeccable as she ironed out the creases and dressed them. Their meals were always seasoned with love. For those few hours Mom spent with them, she made them feel whole. They were her absolute priority. Nothing else mattered. As I watched, I knew in my heart this was my calling, too. I was so proud of my mom. That feeling brought me absolute joy. And when her patients looked at me and smiled, all I saw was love. I knew I wanted to be just like her.

I have been a nurse for over 30 years, and there is not one day that I regret choosing nursing as my career. I started off as a nursing assistant. I have worked in many different places, from doctors' offices to hospitals to clinics. But the places that always pull at my heart are my nursing-home jobs. The demands of working in a nursing home or adult-care facility can be challenging. The pay is often low, and the staffing is often minimal. Yet the work can be rewarding. And nursing assistants are the backbone of all nursing care. I do not think you will find an honest nurse who does not agree with me.

I hope that most nursing homes and adult-care facilities are staffed with only the most loving aides and nurses. I have been honored to work with some of them: those who find pleasure in loving your family and those who will hold their hands, soothe their worries, and caress their frail shoulders. It is happening all over our nation today. They are hard at work, day and night, and I pray for them daily.

Despite this, *you* remain essential to their well-being and continued good care. We have all heard reports of abuse and neglect in nursing homes (or group homes for the mentally, emotionally, and/or physically challenged). Anyone who is unable to speak for themselves and be heard is at risk for less-than-desirable care. Whether it is a caretaker making personal calls during work time or watching their favorite soap opera vs. doing what the resident prefers or outright neglect from poor skin care to lack of response when a resident indicates the need for attention, these things *do* happen. It can even be the person in charge who is either unable or unwilling to call out oversights of staff members. This is why I cannot emphasize enough how important *you* are as an advocate—as an essential person.

According to the dictionary, *essential* means "absolutely necessary or extremely important." That describes *you*. You are essential to them—pandemic or not. It is up to you to find a way to check on your loved ones regularly, because you are essential to them, even more so if they are nonverbal, disabled, or suffering from a dementia diagnosis. Statistics have proven that the elderly placed in facilities suffer from loneliness. Quarantining and isolating of residents have made your job even more difficult. Those extreme measures can contribute to a resident's decrease in physical and mental health and a decline in their cognitive functions.

Select one healthy person in your family to make a visit this week and next week and the next week. Do it. Do not wait. If you are not let into a facility, find out what you have to do in order to visit, and do it. Get the name and phone number of a staff person who will give you a real-time assessment of your loved one. Call them for regular, prearranged video visits. Every essential aide and nurse in the facility has a phone. There should never be an excuse for you to not physically see your loved one. Send cards and pictures to be hung on their walls.

I take heart, knowing that there are many nursing assistants and nurses who are going above and beyond on every shift to do the job they love. I pray that God will give them the good health and strength to continue doing it. I find comfort in writing this, hoping that it moves at least one person to make that call or visit. You are essential. We are all essential, *now* and *after COVID-19*. Never forget it.

The Hole Left Behind

David Seaburn

My first personal loss happened when I was eight years old. My maternal grandmother, who lived with us, passed away. I remember going to the funeral parlor and standing against the wall opposite the coffin. I gathered the courage to walk over to my grandmother and, at first, thought she looked like she was asleep. But after a few more seconds, I thought, *This is not sleep. She is never going to move again.*

During the next ten years, I experienced ten more losses. Some were what might be called in-phase deaths, like great-uncles and great-aunts. Others were not—uncles in their fifties dying of heart attacks, a cousin killed in an automobile accident, and my brother's best friend dead at 16.

It took many years for me to understand how these experiences had shaped me. I know they contributed to my decision to enter the ministry, where the most frequent ritual I conducted for my older adult congregation was a funeral. Later, when I left parish ministry and became a marriage-and-family therapist, I worked for most of my career in a primary-care clinic with patients who faced a combination of emotional and physical health problems. On a few occasions, I was asked to conduct their funerals.

In time, I understood that illness and death were not interruptions to life, but were integral parts of life. No family is immune. Be that as it may, the universal nature of loss does not mean that it is any less tragic, any less jarring. When someone dies, we are faced with a kind of darkness that is often overwhelming. We suffer emotionally and physically. We ask, "Why?" We feel our loved one near us; we may even see them, so intense is our desire for them to return. It takes weeks and months to find our way back to something that approximates normal living. Even then, it is not the same. Nor should it be. The loss of a loved one should change us, stay with us, and make us appreciate the fragile beauty of each passing day, of each relationship, and of each breath.

When I was serving a parish, now 40-odd years ago, the daughter of a close friend died. She had been riding her bike and was hit by a car. She was only eleven—a beautiful, vibrant child. She lingered on the edge of life for many days until her parents faced the decision to remove life supports. We waited until she died. Her physician came to us and said her "spirit was free."

A year later, I asked my friend how he was coping with the loss of his daughter. He told me he had a hole inside that he felt certain would never go away. I was saddened to hear this. He added, though, that he wanted to keep that hole and learn how to live with it, to live in spite of it. His wisdom stayed with me.

Over 30 years later, I wrote a novel about a woman who suffered the tragic loss of her husband and son. There was a point in the story, almost a year after the tragedy, when a close friend tried to comfort her. I couldn't help but remember my friend's wisdom. The character Bobby had just witnessed a buck leaping over a car that was about to hit it. It made him think of his friend Kate.

Bobby swallowed hard. He looked at Kate. "Kate, once upon a time I had a little brother who was three years old. His name was Mark, and I was his hero. We were driving to a picnic on a sunny day, and some guy, coming from the other direction, swerved about three feet, just three feet, and hit us head-on. My mom, my dad, and I—we all made it. But Mark didn't." Bobby wiped the perspiration from his upper lip.

"Sitting there in my truck after the deer had made it to safety, I thought about that accident so long ago. And I realized that while I got to go on living, I was left with a great big hole inside. And that hole bled and hurt and ached for years, and I couldn't figure out how to get rid of it. And people told me that it would go away, that time heals these things, but they were wrong. Time didn't close it up. I mean, it just wouldn't go away no matter how much I wanted it to." Bobby took a deep breath. "And after a while, because you've lived with it so long, it's like you say to yourself, 'You know, that hole isn't going away. In fact, maybe it shouldn't, because if it did, you'd stop remembering your brother,' and you don't want that to happen. And then you think, *Life doesn't go away either*, and you want to keep living, you know, because sometime you might be in the right place at the right time to see a buck jump over a car, or even better, you might see yourself jump over that hole even if it's one time out of a hundred. And you think, *That just might be enough to keep me going*."

Bobby wiped tears on his sleeve.

"Kate, I hope you don't take this wrong, but I think you have a hole inside you. And I'd like to tell you that's it's going to go away, but it isn't. You can't love someone and lose them and not have a hole for the rest of your life. But you know what, you can learn how to jump over that hole, you can learn how to jump over that hole when you need to, you don't always have to fall in. It may take 99 tries before you can do it, but once you do it, you'll be all right—not all better, but all right."

To Laugh or Not to Laugh

Laughter is poison to fear.
> —George R.R. Martin,
> *A Game of Thrones*

Teresa Schreiber Werth

When the novel coronavirus first entered our consciousness, it was as a disease that was raging halfway around the world. It seemed remote, and we seemed safe. As it turned out, it wasn't, and we weren't. As the disease spread and eventually came to the United States, I think we were still in denial. When people started reacting to the perceived threat of the virus, they did it in strange ways, like hoarding toilet paper, of all things! It was about then that I started to receive some pretty humorous e-mails and messages.

Checking my saved photos, I find that on March 19, 2020, I received a photo of two men playing poker, using rolls of toilet paper instead of poker chips. On March 20, I got a brightly colored box with a bold message inside. It read, "To go to the grocery store, they said a mask and gloves were enough. They lied. Everybody else had clothes on!" I howled and passed these gems along to friends including my sister, whom I thought would appreciate them.

123

After a few weeks of sharing many of these zingers, which brought a smile to my face and sometimes made me laugh right out loud, my sister phoned me from North Carolina for our weekly visit. Toward the end of our conversation, I asked her if she had seen the one I sent that day. She paused and said in a careful tone, "You know, I really can't laugh at them." I was stunned. I asked her why. "It's so awful. So many people are dying. I just can't find anything about it funny." I was—uncharacteristically—speechless. I thought I had been helping to brighten the dreary days of the pandemic with some humor, and it turned out, I had not. "That's okay," I quickly replied. "I understand. We process things differently. I won't send them. I certainly don't want to add to your sense of grief or irritate you." And so I stopped sending them to her.

She's an accountant. Everything (by that I mean in her *life*) is neat, about facts and columns and sums. I am a writer. Everything for me is about the moment, the story, the possibilities. We both lead with our heart, but we do it *differently*.

As I thought about our conversation later, I should not have been surprised, and I should have been more sensitive. This was not the first time our processing of issues differed. On the night our father died in a single-car accident in 1997, we drove from Rochester to Buffalo in the dark. I sobbed all the way until my body ached. When we arrived and were comforting each other in turn while standing in my parents' bedroom, our mother said softly, "I'm going to faint." And down she went. She lay there for a few minutes and finally started to come around. As she did, she looked up and said, "Why am I on the floor?" Without missing a beat, I said, "Because you missed the bed."

If my dad had been there, that's exactly what he would have said. He was the proverbial wise guy, jokester. Everybody loved to be around him because he was *so funny*. But that night there was stone-cold silence. This was another moment when my sister and I processed life differently. The joke, the laugh it was intended to evoke, was a release valve for the intense sadness and pressure we were all feeling. But my sister could not laugh—not because she loved our father more or I loved him less or because I was being disrespectful. We just processed that moment differently.

This made me think of a scene in the popular PBS series *Downton Abbey*. Matthew Crawley was killed in a tragic car accident, and his mother's grief was unrelenting. At one point, months after, Lady Isobel Crawley was questioned about her dour mood. She expressed the weight of her grief and said quite plainly that she wasn't sure she would—that she ever *should*—laugh again. She implied that laughing would somehow mean she was over her son's death, that she no longer missed him or mourned him, which was, of course, untrue.

I am still amazed that at funeral gatherings, robust laughter can often be heard—not because it is, in any way, inappropriate. On the contrary, much like the cry of a newborn baby, it is an indication of *life*. Laughter at funerals reminds us that the life we are celebrating, remembering, and honoring is multidimensional, that we share many different experiences, and some of them are, indeed, happy.

None of us knows what the new normal will be like *after* the novel coronavirus. We aren't even sure we will like it. In fact, it's hard to imagine a day when we can say with confidence that this pandemic is truly *over*. In the meantime, each of us is doing the best we can to cope. For some of us that means putting one foot in front of the other, limiting our exposure to the news, and maintaining a routine. Others choose walks and workouts, music, and computer games. Some people pray and worry. Some people escape into books and movies. Some people laugh easily and are grateful for the distraction. Some people find it almost impossible to laugh. We are each having to find our own way because there is no *one* way. We've not been down this road before, at least in any of our lifetimes.

Maybe you saw the movie *Patch Adams* or read Norman Cousins's classic, *Anatomy of an Illness as Perceived by the Patient?* Adams, a medical doctor, believed that laughter, joy, and creativity were *integral parts of the healing process*. He had much success with his approach at the Gesundheit Institute. Cousins, a layman, had a serious disease of the connective tissue that led to him having a lot of pain and trouble sleeping. He found that ten minutes of genuine belly laughter would give him at least two pain-free hours (Cousins, p. 39). Isn't it amazing to think that moments of fun and laughter can bring actual physical relief and healing?

When I read those witty pandemic cartoons and one-liners, whatever is happening in our lives or in the world at that moment takes a back seat, and I am happy. The value of humor lies in how it enriches our lives. I continue to enjoy the cleverly captioned photos although a month after I received the first one, they have slowed down. But in the same way I see buds emerging from brittle branches outside my window, I know we will all be able to laugh again when we are on the other side of this crisis.

Praying for a Better Tomorrow

Ida Pérez

I am sure everyone around the world may be feeling the same as I do. We are all facing the same challenges, the same uncertainties, and even the same fears. Having experienced COVID-19 very close to home definitely puts my personal experience and that of my Latino community in a different perspective.

My brother, Luis; his wife, Pam; and their son, Luis Gary, all tested positive for COVID-19. I felt this was the worst thing that could happen during this time. My sister-in-law was diagnosed first. After being treated at home for the first five days for the common flu, she was finally hospitalized. The next day, she was heavily sedated in order to regulate her breathing. That placed her in a coma for over ten days, a coma from which doctors were having a hard time waking her. They knew that if she did not wake up soon, she would start losing brain activity. All we could do was wait to see if she would wake up…and pray.

In the meantime, my brother was at home, forbidden to be by his wife's side. They had never been separated in 40-plus years together, much less when she was ill and close to death. My heart went out to him. I could not imagine his anguish, his desperation, or his long, restless nights, crying in silence, feeling just as lonely as she did. He was overwhelmed with feelings of helplessness, not being able to be with his beloved Pam. He wanted to be there offering words of comfort to the love of his life, his best friend, his better half, his faithful lover, the mother of his children, and the woman who introduced him and guided him to the love of God.

A week later, Luis was also hospitalized. His symptoms were not as serious as Pam's, but he felt tortured being in the same hospital and not able to see his wife. All we could do was pray.

A few days later, their son, Luis Gary, was hospitalized. Although he was not diagnosed with active COVID-19, it was clear he had carried it and, most likely, had exposed his parents to it. Luis Gary had developed a blood clot in his leg because of complications from the virus. That's what led him to be hospitalized. At that point, doctors believed he had the virus, but unconfirmed.

In the midst of this, I heard another daunting cry. It came from my Latino community. Our Spanish-speaking families, forced to stay home and not fully understanding the severity of the virus, did not know where to look for accurate information in their primary language. Yes, those who had cable could tune in to the national Spanish stations, but they had no idea what was happening locally. Everything was changing by the minute, and it was hard to figure out who needed what and how fast we could get it to them.

I am part of the Ibero-American Action League (Ibero) team, and we knew we had to act fast in communicating to our community. But, most importantly, how could we service them while keeping ourselves and our staff safe? (Did you follow protocols?)

As a not-for-profit agency serving the Latino community for over 50 years, with over 80,000 Latinos currently living in Monroe County, we constantly battle the disparities our community faces.

What we did not expect was how the coronavirus magnified those inequalities. It highlighted the ugly truth of every other entity and the lack of regard for my people.

The first week of quarantine, local news and city and county information all failed to provide information in Spanish and failed to ensure information was reaching everyone who needed to hear it. Ibero took a stand and took steps to make the necessary changes. We offered to translate the information, assigned one of our staff to serve as the city's Spanish translator during press releases and public updates, and translated every article that was written in the local newspaper about the coronavirus into Spanish. We volunteered our own staff to answer 211 calls in Spanish. We ensured that local hospitals, public transportation, and city and county websites translated their information into Spanish. We worked with Foodlink distributing food to the Latino community. We used our Spanish radio station, short videos on Facebook, and other social media to inform our community about the importance of social distancing, washing their hands, and wearing a mask.

Social distancing is difficult for anyone, but when you ask a culture that places the highest value on family and physical affection, it becomes twice as hard. Contacting our elders on a daily basis and ensuring our children were accessing their distance learning became our priorities.

As an agency I'm still not sure if we are doing enough, but I continue to pray. Honestly, praying and being hopeful are what keep me sane. They help me think clearly and allow me to endure all the uncertainties.

I know the power of prayer and hope saved my family and that Pam's recovery was a miracle from God! I also know that prayer alone will not make the disparities facing the Latino community disappear. The new normal can never be what it was before the pandemic. In fact, we need to *ensure* that it isn't. The vulnerabilities of my community cannot be ignored. That is why I will continue to fight for, pray for, and hope for a better tomorrow for my people.

Count It Joy: Making Music in Prison

Catherine Roma

I am writing this essay on the 30th anniversary of entering Ohio prisons to teach and conduct choirs of men and women who are incarcerated. On Tuesday, March 10, 2020, I left London Correctional after rehearsal, not knowing that by day's end Ohio prisons would be shut down to all visitors and volunteers indefinitely. In May we were scheduled to perform five sold-out performances of *The Hamilton Project*, a remount of performances done at Marion Correctional in November. As I grieve the loss of these performances, I am buoyed by the recognition that what we achieved in November has forever changed the lives of all of us who witnessed and produced *The Hamilton Project*. I feel *The Hamilton Project* is the culmination of 30 years of music making that changed my life.

For me, music is the currency of hope and resilience. I have seen this born out working with musicians inside who compose new spirituals. Like their antecedents, these new spirituals are the creative expressions of refuge, spiritual release, determination, and resistance. Out of deprivation and dehumanizing 12×12 cages come life-giving, perceptive, soul-saving, spirit-filled expressions of hope and resilience. These composers write for the same reasons their forebears wrote: to keep their communities invigorated with a relevant song, to comment on their enslavement with code language, to tell their story, to keep hope alive, and to inspire others to hold on.

Quincy Jones wrote a tune, "What good is a song if it cannot inspire, if it has no message to bring?" In reviewing song titles written by composers inside, it is evident, even without hearing them, that songs are a subversive delivery system of faith, hope, and courage. Singing under 24-7 surveillance empowers creators to sustain agency and gain control over oppressive conditions. "It's a New World" by Eddie Robertson was written in 2008 when Obama was running for president: "It's a new world we want to live in, it's on us, it's on us to make a difference, yours and my world, we have the power to make a change."

"By Your Side/Ubuntu" captures Guy Banks's understanding of community: "My friend, you need a hand? I'll be there to help, I love you like I love myself. You need food? We gon' eat together. You take a loss? We gon' grieve together. Forever I'll be by your side."

In "Let's Go Make History," Eddie Robertson sings: "There is a light in you that shines with the light in me/Together we're burning bright, let's go make history/United we can't go wrong, our strength is in unity/Together we can win the fight, let's go make history."

Carceral composers control space when they create. And when there is air to breathe, they change it. Singing the truth empowers musicians to tell their story in a brave space. I have witnessed this music making inside prisons for 30 years, and I am in awe.

As if by magic the opportunity to perform *Hamilton* presented itself. Though not written by men inside, Lin-Manuel Miranda's effective story resonated deeply with the singers. The relevance of the story connected directly to their lives.

"Who Lives, Who Dies, Who Tells Your Story," the last song in *Hamilton*, tells the story of America then, told through the lens of America now. Nothing was lost on the men who performed *The Hamilton Project* last November. It was not just the music they loved that captured their vitality, rhythmic energy, and aesthetic sense or the experienced actors who branched out with newfound skills or the directors or the very welcomed women leads, but it was also the organic goodness and love that reverberated so deeply for everyone in the cast and the 700 outside guests at four sold-out performances, all captured in the pièce de résistance: reflections from *inside* Marion after the show:

> *The Hamilton Project*, the most humanizing, the most humbling, prosocial, rehabilitative, reformative, and collaborative work I've been immersed in, in or out of prison… If only for 85 minutes of my life, I was not a loner, civilly dead. I can proudly say—with my head up and my shoulders back—that I was an addition to my community. (Aaron Burr, played by Scienze)
>
> I tried to find ways to connect to the story, and I did. The "from the bottom" narrative stands out the most to me. Alexander Hamilton had a rough upbringing, even worse than my own. My father left me when I was just a kid, but I had a mother who did her part, to the best of her ability. I was never orphaned, but very much underprivileged. People believed in Alexander's potential to be great and invested in him so he

could have a better life. I'm experiencing that right now, and it feels like a dream. He wanted to contribute something great to society and built a legacy ("something that's going to outlive me"). I want exactly that, and I know that I'm a person who has been given that type of responsibility. "To whom much is given, much is required." I don't possess monetary wealth, but I have vision, intelligence, and talent, among other things that I am supposed to be using to build integrity in this world for the next generation. Therefore, I can choose generativity or stagnation. My legacy will consist of what I did for others. I also realize that I must find balance between family and passion. Alexander missed that opportunity, and I can learn from his experience. (Alexander Hamilton, played by Tron)

Any and everyone who is compelled by the story of America, after *The Hamilton Project* performance, must be compelled by the rebellious aspirations of today's American underclasses. On the other hand, the story also speaks to me and people like me. I grew up in a home and community (ghetto America) in which the concept of patriotism was the farthest thing from us. We saw the government and its representatives as opposition and obstacles. Even today, sitting in a prison dorm as my family struggles and wallows in poverty without me, it's hard not to spend a good deal of time critiquing and condemning this country. However, this musical displayed the marred, but still amazing, beautiful American core. It showed how, even in all its flaws, America is about fight, freedom, growth, and change—all these beautiful things. This performance calls the poor and marginalized to patriotism—not passively ignorant patriotism, but perceptive, aggressive, optimistic, and persistent patriotism.

This experience reconciles people from the top and bottom of our social spectrum. I like this reconciliation because it's not blind "pie in the sky" reconciliation. It calls the top and bottom to unify in full realization of our social circumstance and in that old-time American fight for a better world. And it is super fitting that all this happened in a venue where the free world and the prisoner met to share. What I'm saying is that as I sat in the back of the chapel, I saw the prisoner and the free sharing the greatest artistic expression of reconciliation I have ever seen. (Reflection by resident of Marion Correctional, aka Poo)

Four months after *The Hamilton Project*, as COVID-19 raged inside Marion Correctional, the epicenter of Ohio's prison outbreak, Guy Banks (who played Hamilton) penned the following poem. Perhaps, he was inspired by outside cast members and friends of *The Hamilton Project* to write.

Improvisation/Rap/Poem

Guy Banks (Tron)

I have often felt disconnected to those who don't share the same
struggles I endure in life

I say to myself

they really don't do much on our behalf
at least that's what it seems like

lord knows I was wrong, because when the world suddenly stopped
on us
I seen them take off as soon as they got the green light

it was machine like

they didn't sit on their hands in the comfort of their home

no

they said

what's the next best move
then they did what doers do
blessed with love and food

that's a haiku

peaceful protest and drive byes
emails full of prayers and hope

these are my people on the outside
that are not scared to rock the boat

and what do I see on the on the inside

I've seen men make tea for their neighbors sore throat

nurse them back to health without being certified

they just let
God guide

tell a joke

for the ones who are scared

laughter eases the fear

patience and open ears

are necessary

leaders are necessary

and intercessory prayers

this is
a time
to care

this time will reshape the minds of this generation

a virus declared a war on all of us

kings, queens, rulers, and Presidents, convicted felons all in the same elements.

The only difference is the selfish and the selfless

the strong and the helpless

this is a mandatory thank you

to all of the helpers

who helped us

Loneliness and Grief

Teresa Schreiber Werth

Every act of compassion, kindness,
courage, or generosity heals us from
the story of separation and assures
us that we are in this together.

Charles Eisenstein

You may be surprised to learn that way back in the day (think Vietnam era) disasters like we're living through now were handled by the U.S. National Guard. Eventually, that organization was redirected from providing disaster relief to backfilling combat troop shortages in places like the Middle East. Disaster response was then taken over by the Federal Emergency Management Agency (FEMA) around the time of Hurricane Katrina. FEMA's disaster relief efforts are still around, but after Katrina, the medical portion of disaster response was turned over to the federal Department of Health and Human Services. Under their auspices, the newly formed National Disaster Medical System recruited roughly 3000 volunteers to be divided into task-specific teams of 50 medical and nonmedical personnel who could be called upon to provide coordinated disaster relief in two-week increments.

I have a friend whose team was the first medical team called up to work with Wuhan evacuees and cruise ship passengers exposed to COVID-19. In the past, such teams have responded to hurricanes, wildfires, and earthquakes. Responding to a pandemic was a first.

Each team typically consists of half medical professionals (doctors, physician assistants, nurses, respiratory therapists, mental health counselors, and a chaplain) and half support staff (a commander, an operations' chief, a log chief/record keeper, and security). When the team hits the ground, everyone becomes part of logistics, setting up the operations for the first 48 hours. Then everyone reverts to their specific role. There were almost 400 patients (two groups of about 200) in their camp.

Keeping in mind that these were the very early days of this pandemic, relatively little was known about how it was spread, the range of severity of symptoms, and how to best identify or treat it. Every precaution was taken. Passengers were isolated individually or in couples. Staff were in maximum full protective gear, what we now know as personal protective equipment (PPE). Each person was medically assessed. Everyone with symptoms was tested, waiting several days for test results. The seriously ill were sent to hospitals.

My friend worked very long days in the camp, on the other side of the wall that was the outside world. But she could leave the camp at the end of her 12-hour shift to shower, have a meal, and sleep in a nearby hotel, then do it all over again the next day. She missed her family. They worried about her exposure to the virus. But eventually, everyone was dispatched either to their home or further medical care. And she came home.

When I asked her what the atmosphere was like in the camp, she said, "There was intense loneliness. There was a prevailing sense of constantly being in crisis. There was clearly no fix for what was happening, and the isolation became increasingly difficult for people."

As the days passed and people were sorted out, the atmosphere began to relax a little. Once people were able to be outside—with a mask and practicing social distancing—for a while each day, they showed signs of emotional recovery. People were able to take part in informal town hall meeting twice a day, where staff would give updates on what was happening at their camp and what was happening on the other side of the wall. It was a time when issues about mail and diets and personal concerns could be asked and answered.

Team members eventually began going into the rooms and having casual conversation with patients. "People were so hungry for social interaction that what was supposed to be no more than a 15-minute visit easily turned into 30 or 45. We were the first humans these folks had been able to speak to privately in 14 days!"

When I asked her what lessons she learned from this experience, it was mostly about recognizing the needs of the people who were suffering the effects of their ordeal: being away from their homes for so long, being physically isolated and disconnected from family and friends, having no familiar routine, and feeling anxiety about what was happening on the other side of the wall. In light of these circumstances, she said, "I would urge teams who followed us to overcommunicate because everyone was anxious about everything. I would stress the importance of recognizing and validating their fear. It's absolutely appropriate to experience those feelings in this situation. I would emphasize the importance of answering questions and doing it as honestly as you can. Try to find out answers you don't know, and when you don't know, say so. Keeping in touch with everyone is important, and don't be afraid to think outside the box to address an issue. There are protocols for much of what we had to do, but without a clear direction, you need to be creative!"

Clearly, these people experienced an enormous amount of loss through this ordeal, and losses manifest themselves as grief. We know that grief weighs heavy on the heart in the best of circumstances. The camp was about as far from the best of circumstances as one could get. Remaining upbeat in this situation would have been unlikely for even the most strident optimist. Every day was another day in uncharted territory that felt no closer to resolution, to a return to normalcy, or to assurance that they had escaped being infected by the virus and would be going home to family and friends. Social distancing is one kind of uncomfortable. Social isolation is much worse. Even knowing that the quarantine is medically necessary doesn't blunt the pain of separation.

Navigating the emotional gyrations, grief, and loss of this pandemic cannot be managed alone. We are all in this together. For whom will you be there? Who has been there for you?

When Denied the Last Goodbye: Making Meaning

Lynn M. Acquafondata

Death, like the rest of life, doesn't always unfold in tidy, predictable scenes—sometimes far from it, especially during a pandemic.

When death comes unexpectedly and we are forced to stay away or can't get there in time, we don't just grieve our family member or close friend, we lament the chance to say a final goodbye in a way that feels right and makes some sense.

We like to imagine an ideal bittersweet ending, surrounded by family or close friends, holding hands, whispering soft "I love yous," sharing words of forgiveness, or having one last laugh. We don't imagine someone alone and afraid in a hospital room with anguished loved ones staying away for their own safety.

We expect predictable rituals like a funeral or memorial service within a set time frame—deeply painful, but comforting, not hurried cremations and online memorials. We take for granted that people can show up to bring casseroles, share memories, and hold us close as we grapple with our loss. We don't imagine difficult choices about when or whether to gather at all.

Seven Elements of Meaningful Goodbye

No matter what the circumstances, key elements are usually essential for a meaningful goodbye. All these are still possible even during a pandemic. They just require a different approach. Our typical death traditions and rituals accomplish some of these objectives without our needing to understand the psychological and emotional details of what is taking place. When we can't follow the usual customs, then understanding the underlying needs and purposes can help us figure out how to create meaningful alternatives or how to offer helpful possibilities to those we are trying to support.

A meaningful final goodbye includes the following:

- Telling the story. Grieving in the presence of others.
- Saying goodbye in words, music, imagery, prayer, and/or ritual.
- Recognizing and honoring the person's life, including the way they made a difference in people's lives and in the ways they have contributed to who we are.
- Recognizing a person's flaws and faults, acknowledging the pain of these flaws, and coming to terms with unresolved conflict.
- Being able to picture the person in a safe space after death.
- Finding meaning and purpose in our own life after a loved one's death.
- Letting go of the illusion that grief eventually ends.

Engaging the Elements of Grief in New Ways

Telling the story. Grieving in the presence of others.

We need to talk about the person, about who they were, and about what they meant to us. We need to talk about what happened, sometimes over and over, to try to make some sense of it. If this can't happen in formal in-person gatherings and visits, it can happen on the phone or online or even in letters or e-mails.

As a grief counselor, I used to tell people I would never lead grief groups online. I believed that people needed to be physically in one another's presence to support one another in grief. And yes, that is the ideal. But then the COVID-19 shutdowns changed our lives. Overcoming technology challenges despite the shortcomings of the screen, people come away from online grief groups, feeling heard and understood, able to face one more day.

Saying goodbye in words, music, imagery, prayer, and/or ritual.

There are many other ways to do this when funerals and memorial services are delayed. Some people create artwork or music. Some visit all the places that were special to the person who died. Some write a letter to that person, expressing all that needed to be said but wasn't. Some people say goodbye in significant and healing ways in dreams.

Recognizing and honoring the person's life, including the way they made a difference in people's lives and in the ways they have contributed to who we are.

In addition to funerals and memorial services, this can happen when we do something to honor the person who died: make a donation to a meaningful charity, create a memorial of some kind, or do something to take care of someone else. Some of these could happen in phone calls and conversations from a distance or online memorials.

Recognizing a person's flaws and faults, acknowledging the pain of these flaws, and coming to terms with unresolved conflict.

Coming to terms with the ways in which people and relationships are not perfect is important. This can be one of the hardest parts of grief and is often avoided, even in usual circumstances. Some relationships cause deep pain and even lasting damage. In these cases, it can be helpful to do this work with the assistance of a professional therapist or counselor. Appointments are available online through telemental health.

Being able to picture the person in a safe space after death.

There is not one vision of what this safe space is. It might be an understanding of an afterlife or the promise of reuniting with the person after death. It might be a sense of peace about a gravesite or the place where the ashes are scattered. It might involve living out the person's values in our own life. It might be an image of the person being welcomed and watched over by those who have already died. It might be a reassurance from the person themselves that they are okay through a sign or a dream or just an inner sense. It might be an understanding that the person has become one with the universe in some way. All these things can happen from miles away or years later.

Finding meaning and purpose in our own life after the loved one's death.

This is a very individual element of grief that depends on one's relationship with the person who died and one's stage of life. It involves coming to terms with changes in roles and relationships and daily activities. Some people benefit from doing this with the help of a professional therapist or counselor. These services are available online through telemental health during the shutdowns.

Letting go of the illusion that grief eventually ends.

Many companies expect people back at work within days. Neighbors, acquaintances, and family advise directly or indirectly that it's time to move on. But even in the best of circumstances, grief for a close loved one can change overtime, but it doesn't end. There is some comfort in that realization. It's okay to hold on to and come back to feelings of loss. Maybe we will find that memorial services six or nine months later will fill a deep need for continuing support that people didn't realize they had.

Saying a meaningful final goodbye is possible when we are denied a last goodbye in person. At the same time a meaningful final goodbye is not the end of grief.

Raised to Pay It Forward

Nancy Kennedy

As a young child living in refugee camps, Nhuy "E" Vo experienced hard times. But she also witnessed the kindness of others and experienced firsthand the concept of paying it forward—something she has never forgotten.

"Eating was limited," she said. "They would pass out food to us, but it was just enough and not enough so you'll escape."

"But the people who were there before us would grow vegetables, and they would leave it for the people who came after them. Then you plant for the people who come after you."

Now as an American businesswoman, Vo, 38, and others like her are doing what they can to help in the common fight against COVID-19.

Vo is the former owner of Salon Vo, a hair, skin, and nail salon in Inverness, Florida. In December 2018, she handed the business over to her ex-sister-in-law, Lisa.

Until the salon had to close as part of the state's stay-at-home order, Vo worked there as an employee.

On April 6, she delivered about 50 cases of face masks and latex gloves—800 masks and 23,400 pairs of gloves to be exact—to Citrus

Memorial Hospital in Inverness. Vo purchased most of it herself, and the rest were donated by other salons that also had to close.

"I was able to purchase a large amount from the company we usually buy from, because the salons were closing anyway," she said.

She said she got the idea for doing this from being taught by her parents to always give back to the community, wherever you live. Vo, born in Vietnam, fled the country with her parents when she was four. "After the war, my parents wanted to seek a better opportunity for themselves and for me. My brother wasn't born yet," she said. "We had to flee the country on a little boat to Thailand. That was our first refugee camp."

They would spend four years in camps in Thailand, the Philippines, and Malaysia before being cleared to come to the United States.

"If you were in a camp, you had to do things in the proper way," Vo said. "You had to apply to see which camp, which country you could go to next—who would accept you."

She said everyone slept under an open-sided tent, and every day each family would get a pail of water for cooking and cleaning. There was a well too, where we could get water and do our bathing there," she said. "There wasn't a lot of privacy."

They were in Malaysia in 1988, and Vo's mom was pregnant. "On my brother's first birthday, August 23, 1989, we came to America," she said, "to Tampa, Florida. I was eight."

She moved to Citrus County in 2003 and opened a nail salon. They plan to reopen Salon Vo once the governor says it is safe to do so.

As for the donation of gloves and masks, "Nhuy was quite enterprising and efficient in collecting gloves and masks from local businesses to make this donation," Citrus Memorial Hospital's chief medical officer, Dr. Raylene Patel, said. "We are beyond grateful for this support."

Vo said the donation has another purpose, in addition to paying it forward. "Every disaster that happens in any country, there's a particular group that's affected," she said, giving 9/11 as an example and the backlash on Muslims who had nothing to do with the attack.

She said, with the coronavirus, because it started in China, some non-Asian people have been treating some Asians differently, as if all Asians were carrying the virus.

This points to the fact that people targeted by racism are shown to experience mental and physical health consequences. Onlookers can play a key role in the seriousness of that suffering with *proven ways* to reduce distress for victims, according to advocates and experts.

For victims of abuse, small gestures from bystanders can go a long way, explained John Yang, president and executive director of Asian Americans Advancing Justice.

"So for witnesses who see a hate incident, especially verbal abuse, even standing next to the victim, without even saying anything to the perpetrator, gives the victim comfort and a sense of protection," Yang said.

"And having more people stand next to them to show their solidarity helps to defuse the situation in a way that we don't want to escalate or have it become physical."

The Bystander Anti-Racism Project advises bystanders to consider their own safety and seek to avoid being targeted themselves. But standing up to an abuser and labeling acts of racism can be a powerful show of support for the victim, the group said. That kind of support may even show the perpetrator their behavior is unacceptable

Rosalind Chou, an associate professor of sociology at Georgia State University, explored the concept of witnesses speaking out against xenophobic attacks in her book *Myth of the Model Minority: Asian Americans Facing Racism*.

"If it's safe—and I teach all my students this, we do an exercise about it at the end of the semester—you support oppression by saying nothing when you know it's wrong," Chou said.

"Even just speaking up and saying, 'Hey, that's not okay,' it goes a long way."

Just physically standing by someone provides comfort, Chou said.

"I'm not a sensitive person—I don't take anything personal," Vo said. "But it's out there, it's happening. I don't think people do this purposely. What I hope people will see is that when something happens, the Asian community has their back. I grew up in America—I don't know anything else."

(Teresa Schreiber Werth contributed to this article. https://www.monash.edu/cultural-inclusion/resources-and-support/bystander-anti-racism
www.advancing justice-aajc.org/COVID)

Remember all the local small businesses that you've asked for years and years to donate and sponsor your sports clubs, school events, organizations, etc?

They're calling in a favour.

Answer the call.

In This Together

Adam Lazarus

Let's get back to work.
Please stay at home.
Stay quarantined.
I'm free to roam!
People may catch it.
COVID's contagious.
I'm an American.
This is outrageous!
Close all the stores.
No, open them, quick.
Start the economy.
I may get sick!
Close all the borders.
No, open them now.
Flatten the curve.
But that isn't how!
The death toll is growing.
The doctors say so.
Look at the data.
The science says no.

I listen to experts.

    I know. So do I.

    How many jobs lost?

How many will die?

    How long should we shelter?

Until it is gone!

    But that could take months.

    We need to move on.

What is your plan?

    Don't have one. And you?

I don't have one either.

    So, what should we do?

Maybe stop arguing?

    That's a good start.

We're in this together.

    Let's not fall apart.

I'm nervous and scared.

What about you?

    I know how you feel.

    It's okay, I am too.

What's the solution?

    Not sure. It's a mess.

But we shouldn't quarrel.

That adds to the stress.

    Respect my opinion.

Please respect mine.

We don't need to agree.

    But we need to align!

Let's work together.

And not be divided!

Let's help the country.

And keep us united!

I don't have the answers.

I don't know who's right.

Why battle each other?

There's a virus to fight!

I'm there for you brother.

And I'm there for you.

Let's help the whole world.

And America too.

I'm in if you are.

I'm in as well.

We'll beat this together.

Let's give it hell!

So, you got my back?

Whatever you need.

Then we will recover.

Together!

Indeed.

Silence on the Eastern Front—February 18, 2020

"And indeed it could be said that once the
faintest stirring of hope became possible,
the dominion of plague was ended."
—Albert Camus, *The Plague* (鼠疫)

Brian Linden

Our old square is empty, shops are boarded up, and a red banner playfully blows from the upper reaches of a stone arch and inspires our town to pull together to fight off the virus.

A few local residents sit on wooden benches, all but their eyes covered in cloth. I do not recognize some of them and cannot tell if they are smiling or frowning under their veils. I tell myself that this cannot be my adopted home. Xizhou is usually alive with the commotion of merchants, farmers, and tourists. And yet today all is quiet.

Lunar New Year is the most raucous time of the year in rural China. The seeming discordance of firecrackers, joyous family reunions, and mischievous children together take on the form of comfort and harmony. It is a time of celebration and hope.

This year is different. Signs are posted everywhere encouraging us to wash our hands, wear masks, and stay away from crowded spaces. The streets are regularly sprayed down with an ammonia mixture to drown out any remnants of the bread stands that closed a few weeks ago. Dogs and cats are often more visible than people.

I feel safe here, however. Even while we all struggle to respond to the impact of the coronavirus, I believe that everyone is trying their best to ensure that the virus is contained and the sick are taken care of. I admire the thousands of doctors who have given up their family time (Lunar New Year is meant to be spent with one's elders) and put themselves in harm's way to help those who are suffering. I only wish that we could do more.

These past few weeks have unfolded in a surreal manner. Our hotels were filled with guests, but gradually, reservations were canceled, visitors cut their stays short, and transportation links were curbed. We are already seeing cancellations extending to late summer and early autumn. And while we are sending out regular notices to our friends and followers, urging them to trust that this is only a speed bump, we are not sure how effective this is. Walking through the empty streets of our village makes last month's zeal seem like a dream.

Fear is common during periods like this. But such concern should not lead to racial antipathy and hasty judgments. While this virus may have struck China first this time, no country is immune to this type of outbreak (see statistics from America's seasonal flu and H1N1). While many in China's foreign community have sought refuge back in their host countries, my wife, Jeanee, and I are proud to be staying, standing alongside our Chinese friends and family during this period of crisis. The Chinese government, in the face of massive economic losses, has gone above and beyond to control this disease. We feel safe here.

And while there have been disruptions to our daily lives, this is also an opportunity to reflect and rebuild. I have taken the extra time to learn more about my neighbors, my staff, and the town that I've called home for over 15 years. I have tackled restoration and painting projects that were impossible to do while we were hosting guests. Though I return to my room each night exhausted, I am content in the fact that our complexes are weathering the crisis and proudly awaiting the return of our guests.

Camus wrote in his novel *The Plague*, "This day. I thought it would be marked by terrible signs—lowering clouds, ominous winds, a crack of thunder... Yet, it is so ordinary a morning that I grow frightened."

Life will return to normal here soon. I admire the solidarity of those around me as we all struggle with the unknowns of this virus. Many from the outside may look at us with concern. I wish to tell them (and you) that the government is doing everything it can to control the spread of this disease.

Here in Yunnan, sunshine warms the days under the shadow of the snowcapped Himalayas. The fields of rapeseed react to the glow and capriciously unfurl their golden boughs to the skies. Unlike Klaus in *The Plague*, with every ordinary morning, I grow less and less frightened.

Note—The Linden Centre was founded in 2008 by American couple Brian and Jeanee Linden in response to the pervasive destruction of China's tangible and intangible cultural resources. The Lindens had been residents in China off and on since 1984, and their respect for China's cultural traditions inspired them to create an alternative hospitality model.

A stay at a Linden Centre hotel is an immersive experience into the rich living communities of China's countryside. Their mission is to promote a more genuine form of experiential and cultural tourism and ensure that their neighbors are able to socially and financially benefit from guests' visits. They do this in a number of unique ways, including the preservation of tangible history via the restoration and repurposing of the heritage sites that house accommodations, the incorporation of the local community into their projects via employment, training and education, and the development of experiential programming that benefits both their visitors and their neighbors. The Lindens remain the only foreigners to revitalize such important national heritage structures in China.

A Protective Bubble

Marjorie A. Smith

In my work as a hospice and bereavement social worker, it's not unusual to hear the phrase, "It's not fair." It's not fair that Mom is dying or that my son is dying or my brother or my spouse. It's not fair that they had to go through this suffering. It's not fair that they won't be here for our daughter's wedding. Focusing on the unfairness of it as someone nears death is a normal reaction to dealing with the loss and a normal part of our grieving process. It helps us begin to realize a life without that dear one physically present. It hurts, but it also begins moving us through our grief by raising those strong emotions and realizations to the surface.

During these days of COVID-19, the virus seems to be flaunting its lack of fairness, even laughing in our faces. All normalcy is gone. All sense of inherent safety in our day-to-day lives is gone. Every day it seems we wake to hear of a new and difficult challenge. The impact hits us with the force of an avalanche. And yet there are glimmers of hope even in catchphrases that plead for "social distancing now so we can all be together later." Those are hopeful threads we can grasp on to help us through the unfairness: there is a *someday*, but not for all.

The added injustice heaped on those facing the death of a loved one is, perhaps, one of the most devastating and cruel effects of this pandemic—another layer of distress added to an already-disorienting situation. Not only do people face saying goodbye, but they are also, in many situations, unable to be at the bedside to say it. They most likely cannot honor and celebrate a loved one's life as they would like. Talk about not fair to the nth degree!

So how does one cope if you are facing this cruel reality? How does one make sense of all that is happening when rules for the greater good cause irreparable, painful harm to the individual?

I do not know. I cannot begin to know how people who have lost loved ones, either amid COVID-19 or because of COVID-19, will reconcile the pain they feel because of circumstances far beyond their control. Each of us travel a different path of grief, influenced by who we are, who we have lost before, and how we have lost them. We cannot walk the path these people are on. What I can offer is an honest and heartfelt look at my own experience that may offer some insights.

Loss of control and order in my life was the challenge I faced a few years ago when grieving for Elise, a dear friend and mentor. I felt my world literally spinning out from under me. I had no grounding, nothing to hold on to for emotional footing. For several weeks, I would get up in the morning, sit on the couch, and simply stare at the TV. The loss overwhelmed me to the point that I questioned everything I thought I knew about myself: my beliefs, my approach to life, and my very sense of self. All I could do was rehash the last weeks of her life. In my head, it was like a bad, black-and-white, horror movie playing in a loop without sound. I had never experienced such a devastating loss.

The lack of closure I had surrounding Elise's death contributed to the devastation I was experiencing. I was not with her when she died. There were no services, and her next of kin ended all communication the day Elise died. There was nothing to help me manage my grief.

I was in shock. It is a natural defense mechanism of the human body, brain, and soul to create a protective bubble around ourselves when we face something we consider *unfaceable*. Everything was dulled, grayed, and muffled. Thank God for shock! I was aware that the loss was painful as hell, but the sharpness was softened a bit by my bubble. I couldn't really touch the core of my pain. This state of inertia allowed me time to simply vegetate and regain some of the emotional strength that was drained from me in the weeks before Elise died.

Those days and weeks really are a blur. I do not remember much of them—another effective defense mechanism for my psyche. At a snail's pace, I began reaching out for help, telling people what was going on, why it was going on, and that I was totally lost.

During those days, I lived a moment at a time, sometimes doing okay, sometimes not. I believe what helped me to begin moving out of my bubble was not only *reaching out*, but also *letting in*. Even when I might not have recognized another's attempt to *just be there* for me, it did make a difference. Allowing that person's presence was what eventually broke through the wall of shock. Repeating the story of my pain over and over and over to those willing to listen began to move it outside of myself. Releasing my grief freed up space for my soul and self to expand again. I believe the connection, the human interaction, was the most important impetus for my progression through those hard, dark days.

There is no way to fix what has happened to so many people during this pandemic, no way to set it right. People have gotten very sick; others have died. Jobs and homes and businesses have been lost. Education has been stalled. Graduations, weddings, and vacations have been cancelled.

Savings have been decimated. Dreams have been brutally squelched. And still, "the bad guy" cannot be put on trial and made to pay for his crimes against humanity. *It's not fair!*

But one thing COVID-19 cannot take from you, who have been affected by the virus in so many devastating ways, is this: there will *always* be people who will sit with you in your pain, who will accept you where you are in it, and who will walk with you as you find your way. You may simply need to reach out to them.

Following Littia's Lead

Joyce B. Arnold

When I was growing up, it seemed as if spiders were somehow aware of the fact that I was scared of them—really, really scared! I remember waking up in my big-girl bed, and there, hanging over me, was a spider dangling from its web. It persisted in taunting me even as I screamed the death-defying scream of a six-year-old girl. Then there was the time—or times—when a spider was hanging from its web in the doorway of my bedroom, making it impossible for me to escape. This fear stuck with me like a bad itch into adulthood.

It all took a turnabout one day, a few years ago, when I was in the shower. Glancing up as I rinsed off under the steaming water, I saw her! She was huddled in the corner. Our eyes met (I think). Neither of us moved. Clouds of steam rose between us, and at that moment I thought, *Wow! I must look like a naked monster to her!* And she, well, she looked frightened, naked, and vulnerable too—at least in my mind! Now, normally, I would have thought, *She's got to go! She has to be terminated! She must be flushed down the toilet in a tissue, swirling and whirling her way to the depths of wherever toilet water goes!* But something said, "No!" Something in my weird mind said, "If you name it, you claim it! I don't know where that came from, but I decided to *name* her (I didn't even know if she was a girl.) I called her Littia, a friendly, almost whimsical name.

Since that memorable day in our shared shower, I have met Littia in other rooms of my home, *our home*. We share a smile, a hello, and a joke or two. Of course, I do all the talking, but she *is* a very good listener, my spider friend Littia. And it seems we have been talking a bit more of late.

Now what does a spider have to do with COVID-19, you might ask? Well, with this pandemic's devastating effects and stealthy grip come anxiety and fear. As we hear each day about deaths and illnesses and the sorrow and confinement it is causing in our country and our world, we are frightened.

Since fear, panic, and anxiety are no strangers to me, I have learned over the years that this is *absolutely* one of those times to use my best defense, my strongest ally, and my go-to safety net: humor, laughter, and offbeat ideas not only to lighten the mood, but also to hopefully bring others along.

The first reality I was forced to acknowledge in COVID-land is that I am in the category of "senior with a preexisting condition." Wow! That's a reality check and, if I'm being honest, a bit hurtful. But since most of my friends fit into that category, I thought we could maybe do a senior Zoom (which sounds kind of awkward) or, better yet, talk in a senior way on the phone. And it's happening! I now meet regularly for cocktail hour and a chat with friends here and in other states. I also find that when I do venture out in public, wearing my mask, the lines in my face are less visible. I have my attractive dark glasses on, my baseball hat hiding wisps of gray, and those flesh-colored gloves keeping me safe while covering telltale age marks (aka sunspots). So put that all together, and frankly, I blend right into the COVID crowd and (in my mind) look *pretty hot*, maybe like an *attractive* bank robber—okay, a *seasoned* bank robber?

And I was telling Littia the other day that she was not the only one climbing the walls. Some days, I admit to her, I too want to hide in a corner until things go back to normal. "Normal? Who knows what *that* will be like?" she says.

Littia says she likes to move from room to room—a kind of change-of-scenery thing—and I took her advice. So we, my trapped husband and I, go for car rides from time to time for a different view. We usually pass three or four of his favorite golf courses, where he looks longingly at the lush empty greens and fairways, where no cart has left its tracks in the soggy soil, while his newly cleaned golf clubs wait patiently in our garage.

Our days have become a routine—sometimes busy, sometimes boring, and sometimes just frustrating or sad. And when you have a dog, well, he usually has all the answers, at least temporarily. "Let's go for a walk! Let's play ball! Let's have a biscuit and a beer!" And his big, black eyes seem to say, "Just be glad we're together in this even though we miss our hugs, our family and friends, and yes, the freedom to come and go without hesitation or fear. We're here... together."

And, of course, I have my friend Littia who reminds me often to face my fears and trials with a smile and as much laughter as I can muster while learning to climb the walls properly (even if I don't have that cool sticky stuff on my feet like she does!)[2]

---

[2] Joyce Arnold contracted and recovered from COVID during the pandemic.

Relax, Release, Receive

Bobbi Williams

Imagine a time when animals and humans spoke a common language. There is a belief that such a time truly existed, a time when we spoke freely with four-legged and other creatures. In today's world, what a comfort it would be to share our musings with our pets and to hear their wisdom, knowing they love us unconditionally. The bond between us still exists in a very deep way—words are not necessary. If we learn to observe them the way they instinctively observe us, a soul connection grows.

We believe we adopt our pets; we find them, rescue them, and bring them home. The reality is, on a deeper and more mysterious level, our pets find us. They arrive in our lives to teach us about love and about death.

During the COVID-19 quarantine, animal shelters emptied. Their four-legged residents—mostly cats and dogs—were liberated into the lives of families and individuals. How fitting that at a time of uncertainty and isolation, our animal companions show up to soothe our souls.

When we come home, our animals greet us with a burst of love, and for just a moment, we relax, release, and receive that love: *relax, release*, and *receive*—the three r's of meditation and prayer. How beautiful it is to be present to this.

As we busily text, talk on the phone, get emotional over the news, or find ways to laugh, our animal companions watch us carefully with an open heart. They find comfort in our humanness, our energy, and our voices. They fall in love with our song. They are by our side—constant and unconditional.

Dog walks are shared adventures, a chance to escape and to feel the wind and sun, any weather, but the key is *together*! You can feel the happiness traveling through the leash to your core, a live wire of electric energy. Although you are wearing a face mask and maybe gloves, you two are communing with nature, healing and free.

And when they pass, they teach us about death. Their death makes us realize we have acquired a new room in our hearts. The emptiness we feel still holds the love we shared and waits for the next occupant. These are lessons of the heart of the highest order.

With the full quarantine two weeks away, my lesson about death happened. I have owned five dogs and two cats. Saying goodbye to my dog Quincy was the hardest of all.

We adopted Quincy when he was four months old. A long-haired dachshund mix, he weighed just four pounds and had large, horizontal puppy ears that made him look like an airplane. He was the runt of the litter. His siblings had been adopted; even his mother had found a home. He was being carried around, peeking over the shoulder of a heavyset woman who explained he had been sick at birth and spent most of his early days bottle-fed at the vet's. We brought him home.

Quincy was so happy, playful, easy to housebreak, smart, and a tad protective. By the age of two, that tad grew into full-out fear aggression. He would inexplicably become aggressive as if he no longer recognized us or those he previously trusted. We mobilized to help him with a behavioral vet, medication, a trainer sensitive to his needs, a pet sitter for special-needs dogs, a dog walker, aromatherapy, and anything else I could think of and, most of all, as much love and attention as we could give. We committed ourselves to making a stable home for Quincy. He was pure joy 90 percent of the time. When he had an episode, we knew what to do.

Seven years later, Quincy spun into a storm that made us realize we had enabled his suffering. In fact, we were *all* suffering. It was time to love him enough to release him from these traumatic cycles, having witnessed the worst.

Quincy trusted and loved me. It was the most painful goodbye I had ever experienced. Quincy taught me that it takes courage to love enough to let go, to know that I will feel more pain than he will, and to have faith that he was whole in spirit. The greater pain for us was to live without him, but the greater pain for him was to continue to suffer. This was my lesson of the heart.

During the quarantine, we are hearing about death and love. We recognize that heaven and earth are connected more than ever with prayers and souls traveling Home.

We often think of loved ones as angels watching over us once they have crossed over. It is not surprising to think of our pets as guardians in spirit. I still feel Quincy's presence while walking our other dog.

In ancient times, animal spirit guides were trusted to assist us in time of need. The characteristics of the animal's instincts would be gifted to us to help us find our way. Even now, some sense animal-spirit protection and want to know, *What animal is guiding me?* I read of a woman in chemotherapy who sensed a female wolf arriving during therapy. The wolf brought companions. During chemotherapy they ran ferociously in a pack to destroy the cancer cells. Animal spirits, like guardian angels, arrive in a time of need. They empower us with their will to survive.

Our connection to animals is as old as time and as everlasting into the future. Through them we find the healing power of all of nature. The earth continues to turn and to heal with every season. Animals lead us to nature.

There were times, waking up in the early hours, troubled by some unnameable worry, I would find my dog, curled up sleeping. I would gently, quietly lie next to him and feel comforted by his presence. A calm would come over me as I became present to the simplicity of his love. I recall Wendell Berry's poem, "I come into the peace of wild things who do not tax their lives with forethought of grief. I come into the presence of still water. And I feel above me the day-blind stars waiting with their light. For a time I rest in the grace of the world, and am free."

During this time of pandemic, we are forced to slow down long enough to understand the freedom and healing of nature, the meaning of love and death, and finding peace. Our animals lead the way to show us the peace of wild things.

Returning to Battle Mode: A Veteran's Perspective

Steve McAlpin

Two images were posted on Facebook by a veteran friend as the coronavirus pandemic took hold of the United States. The picture on the left showed people panicking as a grocery store was running out of toilet paper and food. The other picture showed a veteran's legs resting on a porch railing while he was holding a cold beer. The caption read, "This is how veterans deal with a crisis." Not to make light of the current pandemic, but the side-by-side images did force me to smile.

The picture suggests that veterans have been through tougher scrapes. During a frustrating moment on a 2017 trip to Europe to retrace our war years, my good friend Bob (Great Depression and WWII combat veteran) and I clashed over map directions versus GPS guidance. Putting everything into perspective, I told him, "Bob, at least they ain't shootin' at us again!" "I guess you're right, Stevie," he said as he folded the map. "It could always be worse, couldn't it?"

Bob will soon be 95 years old and is in exceptionally good health. He misses driving his car to the gym three times per week, shopping, and attending classes especially for seniors at Rochester

Institute of Technology. His daughter and friends shop for him, and he is thankfully Internet and Zoom savvy. He spends his days writing his memoirs and planning on taking/teaching future courses. "Gotta keep moving, Stevie!" he often tells me.

Bob and I are fortunate that we have, indeed, been through tougher times, but that does not diminish the intensity of this crisis for others, including veterans. We are just a subset of American culture who have witnessed and endured horrific and unforgettable things through service and wartime. But we are just like everyone else when it comes to the basics of life including affection, socialization, independence, and joy. No human being enjoys having their back to a wall—especially when it could be a matter of life and death.

With this in mind, veteran suicide and homelessness are some of the results of post-traumatic stress disorder (PTSD). The coronavirus intensifies everyday concerns experienced not only by veterans, but also by the general population. A comprehensive list of these maladies would be impossible to complete. But as a veteran, I have experienced the gambit of roadblocks from walking with a cane to stuttering to having nightmares and flashbacks, to anger, to the inability to concentrate, and to being in dysfunctional relationships—the list goes on and on. I try to maintain the perspective that I have risen above some of these things, and I will continue to grow.

The coronavirus pandemic has forced me into a battle mode of sorts, realizing that I am well trained, resilient, and willing to accept whatever happens to me. And as a veteran, I am prepared to fight, hunt for food, plant a garden, purify water, build a shelter, and protect my family and community. That is not true for all of us, just me. Many people, including veterans, are quarantined in nursing facilities, unable to see their loved ones and depressed that the freedoms and safety they have paid for in sacrifice and blood are now compromised.

Some of my veteran friends think that this is the initial salvo in a global war. China and other countries have been making great leaps forward to create artificial islands for air bases, infiltrating neighboring countries like the Philippines, and spending a great amount of their massive GDP on military training and armaments. The United States has sunk into massive debt, economic depression, and panic over this unseen enemy, and this is only the first volley.

This pandemic is not a struggle of pain and sacrifice for me. In fact, I have tried to see it as an opportunity to give back. I have come up with a plan to let seniors and veterans, in particular, know that they are appreciated and not forgotten. All I can really do is show my respect *as a veteran to other veterans.* They have done so much for our country to get us where we are today. Without them and their sacrifices and struggles over the years, we wouldn't thrive in this great country.

Recently, I reached out to several senior care facilities around the county, arranging a visit. The staff and residents in these facilities deserve great respect. At the agreed-upon time, I go to a facility in my full-dress uniform. Veterans, staff, and other residents are gathered at windows and doorways. Some gather outside. I render an extended military hand salute to the veterans, seniors, and staff. It is a simple, but powerful image, especially for veterans. I draw my heels together at a 45-degree angle, stand up straight, and slowly raise my right arm to offer a hand salute. That is called present arms. After several minutes, my salute slowly descends. I did that at six locations last week. I plan to make more visits like this, hoping to lead by example. Residents offer waves, smiles, tears, and thank-yous and, of course, a few salutes and flags waving in return—not a dangerous hug or handshake, but a connection of the heart.

Veterans are a large part of the at-highest-risk demographic in this pandemic. My mission is to be sure they know that they are also among *the most appreciated!*

Living in Bubbles

Marina Steinke and Teresa Werth

My friend lives alone in a sturdy, picturesque cabin in the woods in the Finger Lakes region of New York State, an area she chose for its Appalachian-like flora, fauna, and creeks, having lived for many years in apartments in urban areas. Prior to the shelter-in-place rules, she stayed active with numerous friends and activities, considering herself somewhat of a Luddite at home, eschewing TV and most media, while staying in touch with many friends and organizations on the Internet. Until recently, she hauled water from a spring up the road for drinking and continues to use a woodstove as her primary heat source. She remains very connected to the land and the spirits she shares it with, and until a few months ago, she had always had at least one pet for company. She also spends much time in the summer canning, freezing, and drying fruits, vegetables, and herbs for the winter. She shared that she did not have any fears of food or financial shortages as she had always planned for a time such as this.

After a few weeks of confinement, my friend told me that she felt as if she were "living in a bubble inside a bubble inside a bubble" as if time and space had become distorted, and these bubbles not only afforded her some kind of protection, but also served as filters between her internal and external worlds. The smallest bubble held her body and soul, and the next bubble was her personal space at home and within the boundaries of her property, and the largest bubble held the rest of the planet with all of its inhabitants' joys and sorrows. The bubbles also seemed to provide a measure of peace allowing her to withdraw from external events while processing the loss of human contact, a frequent source of sadness and loss. Eventually, she began to not only see, but also feel the filtering effects of these bubbles as she began witnessing the painful events all around her, but did not feel invaded by them. And at the same time, she began to meditate each day, using each bubble as a magnifying lens for sending peace, compassion, light, love, and a feeling of belonging out to all those beings and spaces trapped in darkness.

It was an apt and brilliant metaphor! It was very visual and seemed to convey the boundaries she was experiencing. She was not expressing negative emotions, just observing the landscape of life from an internal perspective. In some ways, she seemed to find it comforting to be living within those bubbles of protection!

Then I heard a news story about the bubble method being used in New Zealand to combat the coronavirus. Could it be that my friend in New York and my friend in New Zealand were fighting the virus in the same way? And so I sent an e-mail to my friend in New Zealand, "Please tell me about the bubble method."

"The bubble method," she wrote. "Well, we were advised (by the New Zealand government) to form a bubble and stay within it—to not have any contact with anyone outside our bubble. Usually, each household formed a bubble. Our bubble was—and still is—hubby, myself, and two of our children. We are a family bubble. People flatting (living in flats or apartments) formed a bubble with their flatmates if there were four or less people flatting together. If there were more, roommates formed a bubble, cooking and eating to be done in separate lots, not in common rooms, bathroom to be sanitized before being used by a member of a different bubble."

It all sounded very civilized and intelligent since the goal was to keep a virulent virus from spreading from person to person. What about people like my friend in New York who lived alone?

"People living alone were allowed to form a bubble with one other small bubble. Children in shared-custody situations with caregivers living within a few kilometers of each other could form one big bubble. If caregivers lived in different towns, the child had to stay with the same caregiver for the duration," she said.

"One person per bubble was allowed to leave the bubble once a week for grocery shopping. People over 70 were not allowed to enter supermarkets. They were allowed to go for a walk, and anyone could go to the doctor if necessary," she added. The elderly, in particular, stuck to the rules, being most at risk. The only group that flouted the rules were the tourists who were still in the country at the time of lockdown. When they arrived from overseas a week or two before New Zealand closed her borders, they were asked to self-isolate for 14 days. That wasn't met with a high rate of compliance.

All businesses—except essential services—and schools were closed. Everyone else who couldn't work from home had no work.

China had bought up supplies of PPE gear and banned the export of these. There weren't enough test kits to go around. That was and still is a worldwide problem. COVID-19 is a new disease, and many aspects of it are still unknown.

Its own geography—the country is made up of two landmasses called North Island and South Island—also helped. If any place could be described as socially distant, it would be New Zealand, surrounded by stormy seas, with Antarctica to the south. With 5,000,000 people spread across an area the size of Britain, even the cities aren't overly crowded.

It had lots of things going for it. They locked down takeaways and stopped all travel. They were able to *contact trace* the small number of cases they had, *test*, and *isolate* them. New Zealanders arriving home had to be placed under quarantine for two weeks. They also had a compliant (although not always happy) population.

New Zealand's lockdown was one of the strictest in the world, moving from alert level three to level four within 48 hours. On March 26, when there were around 280 cases, offices, schools, bars, and restaurants (including takeaway and delivery services) were completely shuttered. A tally by the Johns Hopkins Coronavirus Resource Center has the number of COVID-19 cases in New Zealand as of May 10 at 1,494; 21 people have died, and there are two new cases. Also on May 10, cases in the United States of America were 1,309,541 with 78,794 deaths and 25,600 new cases.

My New York friend's bubbles were real and reassuring to her. Her cabin in the woods was her safe haven because that was what she instinctively chose. But instinctive, intelligent choices were no match for having a well-articulated plan. New Zealand's bubbles were clearly defined, well orchestrated, and highly effective. There might be a few other pertinent factors: New Zealand managed to avoid the confusion and half measures that hampered the response in many other places. "New Zealand got everything right," said Prime Minister Jacinda Ardern with a sense of well-earned pride. "We had decisive action, with strong leadership and very clear communications to everybody." Their bubbles worked.

Who knew bubbles could be so effective in a pandemic?

School is NOT closed for the year.
The building is.

—

If you listen closely you can
hear the hum of hard working teachers,
administrators, and support staff.
**Yes, we are brokenhearted,
but these broken hearts will lead.**

Shining Stars

Pennie Sue Williams McGanty

I'm a teacher in my thirtieth year of elementary education. Over the years, I have seen many changes in the way we teach to reach every one of our students. Anyone who chooses to make teaching a career knows there are always going to be changes, stress, and the inevitable unknowns. But right now, during this coronavirus pandemic, the changes and stress we're experiencing *are* the unknowns to teachers and our students.

I am getting ready to begin week eight of being an online teacher, a position for which I have little-to-no experience. The stress is real! Yes, I have my second graders use their Chromebooks on a daily basis in the classroom. However, I have never before had to create my curriculum or make online instructional videos, using programs I have never heard of, or hold my daily morning meetings and our once-a-week *Eat in the Classroom with Me* through something called Schoology Video Conferencing. Talk about a steep learning curve!

Over the past eight weeks, I, and teachers all over America, have turned our home dens into temporary classrooms. I have gone into my school building—into my classroom—only once since March 13. I did this to pack up language arts, social studies, and math books and to wipe off boards and markers I might be able to use when making videos. I also packed some of my student's favorite items, like the pillow that says, "Today, I will be kind, be nice, be fair, and be happy." I also brought the students' stuffed bear holding a silver star that says, "Shining Stars," the name I gave my students. I thought having these items visible for the boys and girls during our meeting would be comforting and familiar.

As a veteran teacher, I know my students will continue to learn even though we are not physically together. But I question my ability as well as the quality of the lessons I am preparing and sending my students. Throughout this pandemic, I have often felt like a brand-new teacher walking into my classroom for the first time. I keep reminding myself that I know how to teach. I know how to reach all my students. I know how to integrate technology into all my lessons. Even so, now I can't sleep through the night because my mind is on a constant roller coaster, wondering what is going to be waiting for me when I open my school e-mail or look at my phone in the morning.

I get up to messages from administrators sending updates and asking for data concerning my students' completed activities. There are messages from my students and their parents asking how to open or complete an assignment. We are being given new programs administrators want us to use, programs we have never heard of and had no training on. I am expected to learn on my own, in my family room, how to make instructional videos on *Screencastify, Loom,* and *YouTube*. I have to find or figure out how to create assignments for my students, using *PlayPosit* and *Edpuzzle*. I have cried on a Zoom meeting, in text messages, and on phone calls with my grade-level teachers and friends, not to mention my loving husband, whose ears have been scorched listening to my falling-apart rants. I have decided if tears were pounds, I would be a size six right now!

I have felt like a flight attendant who has been asked to take the seat of the pilot in the cockpit and safely fly and land the plane full of unsuspecting passengers across the Atlantic Ocean to London, England. Just like the flight attendant, who is familiar with the plane and has most likely been in the cockpit, s/he still has little-to-no experience using the instruments needed to do the task s/he has been given.

I am working longer and harder than I ever have before, making sure all the t's are crossed and the i's are dotted. Though through all this I realize that I have grown as a teacher. I have gained confidence and have become a better teacher. I know that I am doing my very best for all my second graders. I know that each one of them is still—in spite of all the changes and disruptions—learning and thriving in their education. I understand, my students are working hard on everything I assign to them.

I have always had a good rapport with my students and their parents. Because of this abrupt change from physical teaching and learning in the classroom to distance/online teaching and learning, I have felt more support and understanding for the role I am fulfilling, especially from the children's parents. I have seen wonderful sides of the boys' and girls' personalities that don't reveal themselves in the classroom. I have met family pets and seen bedrooms and favorite spots in the house through our *Schoology* conferences. I have seen genuine excitement on my students' faces when a student joins our meeting for the first time. I have enjoyed their laughter, their intrigue, and their thoughtfulness toward one another and me.

During our class's morning meeting after spring break, one of my students shared that his family dog had died. All my students told him how sorry they were for his loss as we all shed tears for that little boy. I could feel the love they shared and how much we all were together—but alone.

I know in my heart that all 18 of my wonderful little second graders are working hard and continue to do their very best. They are my shining stars. Even though they too have heartfelt concerns about the coronavirus and their school activities, they are shining brighter than ever. I know they are working hard, probably harder than they ever have, because they too miss the physical classroom.

They will be fine. Yes, they have missed some of the curriculum they should have gotten this year. However, children are resilient. They are ingenious, and learning is as natural for them as teaching is for teachers. I chose to be a teacher many years ago, and because of this very strange, very disruptive, and very demanding moment, I still know it was the right decision for me. I know that I will continue for several more years to make a difference in the lives of children and in my own life! This coronavirus pandemic has dropped a gray cloud over me for now, but it too will pass. I will not let it change what I love and do best—teaching children!

Healing Old Wounds and New Life

Lauren Benton

Growing up queer and closeted, one becomes well acquainted with the constant hypervigilance, sense of isolation, and soul-reaching injuries that come with not only having to protect oneself, but also trying to navigate a world that feels like land mines. For me, that meant that even the spaces that were once safe and affirming were now full of questions, doubt, and fear at best, and full-on psychological or emotional violence at worst.

And I'm one of the privileged ones whose *worst* didn't involve parental abandonment, physical brutality, or death. Even after coming out, grieving the losses of relationships with people who said they loved me, desperately trying to find community, and figuring out how to exist in general now that the target was firmly planted on my back instead of being hidden under my shirt, those original feelings and ways of being were not instantly gone. My heart remembers even now, many years later. Throughout life, certain events activate these scars: ones that have obvious similarities and some that don't seem to correlate at all on the surface. COVID-19 is one of the latter.

I didn't realize it at first, really. Working in community mental health, a good portion of my mental and emotional energy is reserved for the clients I serve. When coronavirus hit, my work with most of my clients shifted to focusing on survival instead of growth, healing, or recovery. Where can they get enough food to quarantine? Since schools are closed, how can they find childcare so they can still go to work? What if the unsafe people they live with become aggressive? And, of course, all these questions are especially complex for my clients with any minority identity because of the oppressive social and political dynamics of our country. In times of stress or chaos, we focus on recognizing what is in their control, but the most concerning problem is that that answer is usually very little for the folks with no or minimal power, resources, or access.

Being nine months pregnant, another large chunk of my energy has been focused on growing a human for the first time and figuring out how to be a (queer) parent, which again come with draining experiences ranging from annoying (i.e., having to cross out *husband* on day-care applications and change it to *parent #2*) to offensive (i.e., health-care professionals not being willing to work with us in regard to starting a family, because they do natural family planning or acquaintances telling us about how it will negatively impact our child to not have a dad). This is the area of life where I first realized the grief that COVID-19 was bringing.

It is traditional in both mine and my wife's families to celebrate new life with events that bring many generations of family and friends together to reinforce the "village" that is going to help support us and the baby. These events had to be cancelled. All our baby-prep classes through the hospital were cancelled. The hospital policies quickly shifted to only allow one support person during anyone's hospital stay, which meant our parents could no longer come meet the baby after they were born. (We are keeping our fingers crossed that my wife will still be allowed to come with me a month from now as some people in other areas had to go through labor and delivery alone.) Half of my prenatal doctor's appointments have switched to five-minute phone calls. The feelings of disconnection, loneliness, and being unseen returned with a vengeance. For safety's sake, we cannot see or hug or sit with that community we have fought to create. Our baby will meet their village through windows or electronics. Pregnancy, in and of itself, at least for me, comes with some fear and anxiety. Put coronavirus on top of that, and it's, "Welcome back, Hypervigilance, my long-lost friend. Cue all those questions my brain used to know well: What do I have to do to navigate the world safely? What if it doesn't work or I make a mistake or it's not enough?"

I am trained to help people manage stress, learn to cope, and work toward growth and healing. Nonetheless, I firmly believe that one of the most helpful things I can do right now is sit with my clients in the chaos (albeit virtually): Tell them that I get scared, too. Tell them their grief is valid even if no one they know has died. Discover how they can feel social closeness while physically distancing. Help them dismiss the societal messages they are being fed about using quarantine time to be productive, organize their living space, or start that business idea that just lead to pressure, distress, and shame. Identify how to problem solve obstacles that are in their control, and when they feel able to, help them connect with something, anything, that gives them even an ounce of solace or hope.

Thus, in true therapist-life fashion, I am challenged to live my personal life congruently with the pillars and values that guide my professional work. Lately, that means I sometimes sit with my wife in the feelings of loss, cry, and validate the pain even though it's not the worst-case scenario. Sometimes that means I remind myself every day or every hour that this virus will not last forever even though we have no idea when it'll end. It means going to my own therapy even though it doesn't feel quite the same talking through a screen. It's recognizing when my scars feel like wounds again. It's putting my hand on my stomach, closing my eyes, and becoming focused on the connection I have with my child. And then it's basking in the incredible awe that comes from realizing how inherently resilient they are, even by existing, let alone being born during a pandemic. They are so brave without even knowing it even though they didn't choose to be—just like everyone else trying to survive the best they can, just like my clients, and just like me.

© Babak Tafreshi

212

We Are

Y.M. Barnwell

For each child that's born
a morning star rises
and sings to the universe
who we are.
We are our grandmothers' prayers.
We are our grandfathers' dreamings.
We are the breath of our ancestors.
We are the spirit of God.
We are
Mothers of courage
Fathers of time
Daughters of dust
Sons of great vision.
We are
Sisters of mercy
Brothers of love
Lovers of life and
the builders of nations.
We are
Seekers of truth

Keepers of faith
Makers of peace and
the wisdom of ages.
We are our grandmothers' prayers.
We are our grandfathers' dreamings.
We are the breath of our ancestors.
We are the spirit of God.
For each child that's born
a morning star rises
and sings to the universe
who we are.
WE ARE ONE.

To listen to this song, go to: musechoir.org/sing-to-the-universe (select Track 4).

Black Female Physician: I Am Not Immune

Teresa Yvonne Smith

I am often judged when I walk into a room, not because of merit or even anything I have said, but because of what I look like: a Black female. I am often told to smile more so that I am less intimidating and more approachable. Suffice it to say, my gender and race carry much more weight in shaping first impressions than the content of my character or the fact that I have three degrees, including a medical doctorate, went to private schools all my life, and come from a middle-class family. Before I even open my mouth, I am judged, often taken for granted: "Are you the nurse?" "When will I see the real doctor?" And yet I am still privileged compared to many of my patients of diverse ethnicities and cultures, who come from the urban communities of New York to travel to our public hospital for health care.

There has not been a time when this was truer than now. Communities of color were tumbled by a pandemic that, at the outset, was seemingly not racist and did not care for color nor stature. However, it was the health disparities that exist within the communities of color, the lack of access to equitable and affordable health care, and the fractured health-care system that allowed COVID-19 to lethally impact the most vulnerable. In fact, most disasters do hit those communities already suffering from social, economic, and health disparities at much higher and longer lasting degrees than others. Those were the families already suffering to care for their health who died in this pandemic—those vulnerable patient populations who often had to make life decisions of going to their weekday doctor's appointment or going to their jobs that paid hourly (thus missed work meant no income), or the all-too-common decision of paying for food or paying for their medications. These populations already faced housing insecurity, lack of healthy food options, and fewer specialized health services. These populations are people of color. So when a pandemic of disastrous proportions attacked the world, those were people of color, struggling to fight against health disparities that succumbed in great volume to this virulent virus.

Within weeks of surviving this brutal virus, those same communities of color faced another pandemic that has plagued our country for generations: racism. For eight minutes and 46 seconds, they watched as callous police officers took the life of George Floyd. We were reminded yet again that Black lives mattered less than all other lives. Just as COVID-19 did not care whose life it took, racial injustice did not spare life either. Those in the communities of color were not surprised by the killings of Ahmaud Arbery, Breonna Taylor, Rayshard Brooks, or George Floyd. Our parents warned us of the very fact that when we left our homes, we left their safety and protection. It was George Floyd's call for his mother that recoiled our hearts and reminded so many people of color that their mother might not be nearby when faced with conflict of racism. Communities of color were not enlightened by the filming of acts of racist terror, but instead were tired and, quite frankly, sick and tired of being tired. These people already fighting an invisible war with a virus ravaging their bodies were standing up for the visible racism calling their bodies worthless.

And what did we learn? How will we do better? As the tide of the pandemic fades in my city, the economic impact rises, and the budget cuts loom. We should be putting more money into fighting the health disparities that led to the disproportionate death from COVID-19 in communities of color. We should be prioritizing funding so that health care is seen as a human right. We should be making health care accessible for all and making sure medical research is inclusive of diverse patient populations. We should be breaking down the barriers and inconveniences that make taking care of one's health difficult, especially if you are poor or Black and/or brown. If we do not address the social determinants of health, we have learned nothing from the pandemic. And yet we hold our breaths to see the aftermath of the most devastating public health crisis of our generation. We, physicians on the front line, anticipate the cycle of healthcare budget cuts where funding is needed most, which will lead to health disparities, inequitable care, and more illness. Thus, the cycle continues. Health-care injustice is the same as racial injustice in that it says Black lives do not matter.

As a doctor, I am not immune to both the virus and racism. I have been accosted by the police after a shift in the emergency department while wearing a white coat with the title *doctor* etched on the pocket and my blue scrubs. Tired, feeling the braveness that exhaustion ensued, I stated, "Officer, please give me a ticket. I deserve the ticket for double-parking. I will take it. But what I will not take is your disrespect." Even donning my doctor's attire, I was reminded that I was still Black, and no degree could make me immune to the racism we, as Black people, faced. And as I teach my patients how to protect themselves from COVID-19, I only pray that we, as a society, will educate ourselves and protect one another from the racism, sexism, homophobia, antisemitism, anti-Muslim acts, xenophobia, and every other plague we all face.

Mother's Day 2020

Teresa Schreiber Werth

Mother's Day 2020 would be, to borrow a cliché, one for the books.

With no brunches and no visits, it was challenging and memorable. It's always one of the busiest days of the year for restaurants, retail stores, jewelers, and florists. This year was different. The greeting-card displays were completely gutted, and florists were working at warp speed. Amazon and other gift card and mail-order companies were buzzing with activity. Even Omaha Steaks had a special Mother's Day boxed set. Talk about sentimental! But try as we might, nothing could replace a face-to-face visit complete with hugs, kisses, and maybe even a few tears. Few moms I know had any of that.

We had to be satisfied with texts, cards, and gifts sent in the mail, FaceTime or Skype visits, and solitary confinement. I watched a sweet video (obviously filmed before the pandemic) of a young woman standing on a busy street somewhere in the south of France. She was blindfolded, and standing next to her on the ground was a sign that said, "Free hugs!" She stood there hugging strangers of all sizes, shapes, ages, and colors, person after person after person for all five minutes of the video—and even after that. Tears streamed down my face as I watched the simple, energizing human connection of hugs between strangers.

I would love to do what she did. It was difficult to realize that if I did that today, it would be a life-threatening act. That's so hard to wrap my head around—how could hugging be mortally dangerous? Life was never supposed to be like that. Would it ever be safe to hug again?

I see our 17-year-old grandson at least weekly. In our family, we're all huggers, but this once-cute little bugger is now 6'4" and towers over me. His hugs are long and strong, and boy, do I miss them!

I am fortunate because I can hug safely all day every day. My husband of almost 50 years is always happy to fulfill my need for a squeeze, and I'm happy to do the same for him. But for my friends (many of them, senior citizen friends) who live alone, it's a real issue. It's a real loss. And like any of the other losses we are experiencing, it feels like grief. We truly grieve our lack of touch, of physical warmth, and of contact.

One of my friends had to have her computer looked at near the beginning of this quarantine. It had only been a few weeks since her isolation began, but she's a hugger and, by her own admission, was feeling deprived. "In fact," she said, "I needed a hug so badly that I almost asked the computer guy if I could hug him!" That's a whole new kind of pandemic-desperate!

Another friend has a daughter who was diagnosed with COVID-19 early on and was very sick for over a month. She is finally recovering. This friend also played a big role in caring for her eight-year-old grandson, Colton. They are very close and love spending time together. His dad, Mike, a police officer, insisted everybody play by the rules in order to avoid this invisible enemy of coronavirus. Early in the pandemic, she could stand by the car and speak to Colton through an open window. She could blow him a kiss. After months of being apart, my friend decided that on Mother's Day, she'd had enough. "I told them they were going to come into my house, sit down, and we were just going to talk." "Are we going to wear masks?" asked Mike. "Nope," she said. "We're just going to risk it. I've had enough. I just want us to be together and almost normal."

And so on Mother's Day 2020, the family came into her home without masks. They all sat down, a safe distance apart, and visited and laughed, and at least for a little while, life felt almost normal. When it was time for them to leave, they walked toward the front door, and Colton grabbed his grandma and gave her an enormous, pent-up, desperate, loving hug. His father cleared his throat and said, "Well, you're not going to get away with that, young man" and moved in to hug his mom too.

As my son would say, *it was a moment:* Mother's Day 2020— one for the books.

Choosing Life

Gloria Osborne

Many of you may look at this title and think, *Really? Who is this person? Of course, we're all just trying to get through this.* But the honest fact is that not everyone has the courage or support they need to make it through this horrible crisis, a crisis that is terrifying for some, overwhelming for others, traumatizing for many, and a real testing ground for most of us. It begs us to grieve for the dead and empathize with their families while we are unable to offer the consolation and support through whatever ritual is a part of their culture. It deprives those who have lost friends and beloveds or those who have stared into a stranger's eyes as they passed from life to death of the reassurance so badly needed. There can be no pat on the back or warm hug or even hand-holding.

Think of all the essential workers—everywhere—worried for their families and fearful of becoming ill. Remember all the undocumented workers who are feeding us, but have not been provided with PPE and will not receive a stimulus check or any other aid. Think about the nonessential workers who are no longer working and have no paycheck to tide them over for their mortgage or rent or food. Imagine how some of them are feeling!

And then there are all the homeless or those being housed in prisons, jails, and detention centers; children separated from parents; juveniles who, themselves, are still children; refugees in camps or on islands they can't escape; or our own indigenous families relegated to reservations with no running water and already suffering from the side effects of uranium mining or fracking on their lands—all with very limited or no medical care. They all have families somewhere, many who care about them as much as we do our own families. And our country's pandemic response is being orchestrated by a government that places greed above the value of human life as they bail out the rich who are making *billions* from this pandemic.

And have I mentioned the chronically ill and aging or those who have just been diagnosed with a life-threatening illness in the midst of such chaos or those whose history of trauma goes so far back, many of us don't remember it, *but they do*? For them, every moment and lack of someone caring or being able to help is a trigger to pain they have suffered their whole lives. Consider too the mentally ill—which includes a lot more of us now—and the demands being made on therapists and counselors who have their own families and lives.

I am sure I have left out many: those who live totally alone, isolated from others, who are navigating this crisis alone, those with only a TV full of lies and rumors or a radio to listen to. How many of them will not reach out for support because of feeling they are a burden on society?

Friends, as this pandemic progresses, many may choose to die, either by default or suicidality, because of fear, isolation, or deep grief. Whatever led people to consider choosing death before this pandemic will certainly increase as a result of it. *Or will it?*

During the first few months of 2020, we have seen the best and the worst of our society. Now we have the best reason in the world to *live*, to choose *life*. We do that by becoming a part of a *revolution* grounded in love and nonviolence, by creating community gardens or sewing circles or talking circles or book circles. For those of us privileged enough to have access to Zoom and webinar programs *in the relatively short space of just these past few months*, we have experienced the inter- and intraglobal possibilities of working together and creating societies that are supportive and regenerative vs. greedy and competitive.

As we move toward the postpandemic world, we have the opportunity to reinvent ourselves one step at a time. Countries can work together and share information so we can, at the very least, be prepared for future pandemics and, at best, avoid them. We can offer every citizen access to the Internet in order to exchange ideas and create more versatile circles from the comfort of our homes or picnic tables. In short, we have a million new conversations waiting for discussion and action—discussions and actions that all of us, regardless of age or ability, can be a part of by simply creating inclusive small circles and sharing with one another out of our mutual compassion.

But how do you begin? It's not really hard. You begin with each circle participant bringing a stranger who can share something new—not the same old rhetoric. Invite. Share. Repeat. And you do this over and over again, embracing one another, extending your reach as the circle grows. Only by lifting one another up, over and over and over again, can we hope to bring light to the darkness.

Our Bones Remember

J. Dawn Knickerbocker

As I write this, 100,000 people have now died of coronavirus in the United States. The virus came to us in winter, during the hard and cruel months, taking the most vulnerable. It stayed with us in spring while the sap began to run from trees, while the buds silently emerged, and while storms shook the earth and flooded fields. It took the people by surprise and forced us into isolation. It is now the beginning of summer, and the air is heavy, hot, and filled with uncertainty. In our Ojibwa language, we call this time the *zaagibagaawi-giizis*, "the second of 13 moons," which is a miraculous time of year when there are supposed to be renewal and growth. The virus is still taking us.

I am *anishnaabe-kwe*, which means that I am "a woman of the original people of this land." I reside in the small village of Yellow Springs, Ohio, where my ancestors traveled, but the tribal council fires no longer burn here. I've had to find my own way and remember the lessons of how to live—especially how to live in a time of uncertainty.

COVID-19 has devastated Native people.

I listen to the news sounding the alarm that Native Americans are particularly vulnerable to the spread of COVID-19. Reporters write that we are more susceptible to dying from this disease. Historically, we are not strangers to infectious diseases. For many of us, this is triggering of trauma remembered. Nearly all the population areas of the Americas were reduced by over 90 percent because of disease. It is the most extreme population decline this land has ever witnessed and will ever witness again, hopefully.

And so it goes, our Native Nations are no strangers to the danger a pandemic can pose. Our bones remember. I remember.

Giga-waabamin menawaa.

In my language, Ojibwa language, it literally means that "I will see you again, and I still see you even when you aren't there." This phrase reminds me of the resilience and strength of my people. It reminds me that we do not forget, but instead, we learn and are hopeful as we move from season to season, from generation to generation.

I am thankful that my ancestors and family have passed down survival mentality as normal. We grew up with stories of smallpox blankets—entire families gone, but one or two survivors. These stories were told in quietness, barely uttered.

Our heroes were people who could ride without a saddle, who could forage food or train their dogs only using hand signals, in complete silence. We learned to sneak through the woods, ride bareback, swim without ripples, sleep outside, and get up before light. It was a part of life. It was joyful and normal. We learned to be cautious, quiet, and kind, hoard supplies, grow our own food, share with people we could trust, and use restraint with neighbors we didn't know.

Things and stuff are not important to us, and wealth is ultimately temporary. What is important to know is the land you live on or near and to love it. Appreciate fruit when it's ripe. Let the children play in the rain. That's what's important. We also learned that there are only two lasting sicknesses: being unprepared and being in anguish alone. These cause the most harm to our lives.

What's happening globally during this pandemic is heart-wrenching, swift, and deadly. For many indigenous communities, the politics and effects of this disease are nothing new—that's a hard truth. Our strongest communities are learning to survive and rely upon one another, to stand firm as our own best advocates.

As the summer sun warms the earth, it is the time of renewal and growth. We are learning to remember our ancestors and the lessons they placed in our bones—to keep us resilient and grateful for each day we are here.

And for the 100,000 who are now gone, *Giga-waabamin menawaa*—I still see you, remember you, and will learn from you.

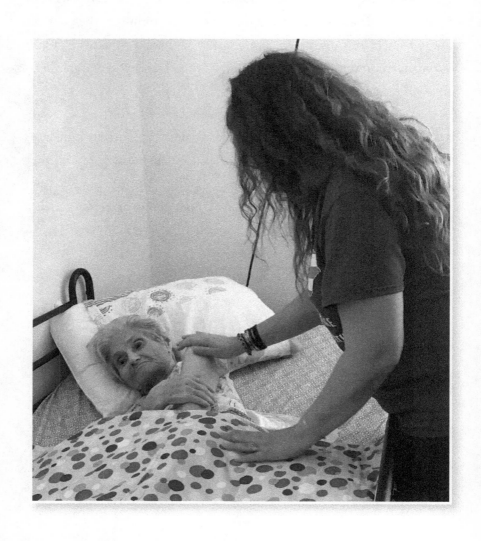

Love Will Find a Way

Teresa Schreiber Werth

I worked as a volunteer at a local two-bed hospice for five years after I retired. A friend and I took the Monday night shift from 7:00 to 11:30 p.m. It was a peaceful time in the house and very different from the bustle and activity that often accompanied the day shift. In the evening we gave medications and logged them in the resident's chart, read to them, put on a CD if the resident enjoyed music, maybe lit a candle, and often sat by their bedside and visited. It was always interesting to hear their stories, but sometimes they just wanted someone to sit quietly and hold their hand. Nobody wanted to die alone, and our presence assured the family that someone was always there with their loved one.

One blustery Western New York winter evening our on-call hospice nurse told us that one of our residents, a very sweet little woman we'd been caring for, for a few weeks, was going to die very soon. She asked me to call the woman's husband and ask him to come right away. The roads were slick, and the wind was howling. It would surely be a treacherous trip even though he didn't live far away. I kept watching out the front windows. When the headlights of his car finally swept across the snowy parking lot, I went to the front door and opened it. He stepped in carefully. "I'm sorry," I said.

"She's gone." It was one of the saddest moments of my life. Through no one's fault, he didn't arrive in time to say goodbye. The hours he spent with her every day spoke volumes about his love and devotion, which she surely knew after so many years, but he missed that last chance to say it one more time, and nothing any of us could do would change it.

As the pandemic of 2020 rages, people struggle with the possibility of not being with a family member or friend as they fight, and eventually succumb to, the virus. They agonize about not being able to be present at death and not having one last chance to say "I love you" and "goodbye," to forgive, or to make amends. Some folks have gotten creative and found ways to have *one more time*. The media love these stories because they feel like little victories over the virus as people find ways to (safely) defy their forced separation.

There is the old-fashioned method of writing a love note. You can be as serious or silly as you want. Just print on the person's name on the face of the envelope along with, "Please open and read this to her/him immediately!" Sometimes staff in the chaplain's office will help facilitate this.

Some people have been successful asking a member of the staff to hold a cell phone or iPad close to their loved one so they can speak to them or see them and maybe even hear a response. Leaving a message, poem, or song as a voice mail is another way for someone to send their love, and it can be listened to many times. Some clever people have been able to sit in a lawn chair outside a first-floor closed window and be heard, hold up notes, read lips, or do some panto-mime! I saw one news story that involved a ladder enabling a person to reach a second-floor room window—probably not the best idea, but desperate times called for desperate measures. I have even seen messages written on the pavement in chalk and singing or instru-mental groups outside a patient's window.

As the crisis escalates and staff become more stressed, resources are scarcer, and everyone is trapped in a strange, uncertain world for an unknown time. Being able to successfully make these remote con-nections becomes increasingly difficult. This is not because medical professionals don't care about your suffering and separation. On the contrary, during every long, hard shift, they are pouring themselves into saving as many people as they can, including someone you love.

And when that dreaded phone call comes, that your loved one has died, your chances for being able to express your love one more time and say goodbye evaporate…forever.

Your sense of grief and loss may increase exponentially. That, combined with the fact that the rules of the pandemic prevent you from gathering together as family and friends to remember, mourn, and celebrate a precious life, can blanket your life with darkness. Those are all very normal and appropriate feelings, along with anger, helplessness, and depression.

Affirming those feelings is one of the healthiest things you can do. Hiding or suppressing them can be dangerous. Seeking profes-sional help is one very good option. Doctors, therapists, and clergy are experienced in helping people through these difficult times. Seeking help is not a sign of weakness, but a sign of strength as you intentionally take control of your life.

Someone I know who lost her father to COVID-19 chose to respond creatively to her unbearable grief. Around her home and office, she put together small collections of items belonging to her father. She told me they were little altars of things that reminded her of him: his luggage tags from trips they had taken together, his gavel from his time as president of his Rotary Club, and the golf ball from his hole in one. She had a pine-scented candle in one grouping and his coffee cup, some incense in another along with a special pair of cuff links, and some rocks they had gathered when they visited the Southwest. Sometimes, it's the ordinary small things that bring us the most comfort and that are enormously infused with meaning.

"All creation is precariously contained in a mended cup of meaning," writes Nick Cardell. "It is the cup from which we drink our lives, the cup with which we drink *to life*. It is the cup that is broken and mended, broken and mended, over and over again. Each time an era passes, a way of life is destroyed, or someone of significance to us dies, we cry out that our cup is broken, and so it is. Yet, somehow, together, we must find, we do find, the way to mend it all over again."

Love will find a way. It always does.

Closure and Celebration

Marina Steinke

We are facing troubled times caused by a tiny organism that has infiltrated our society. We are defenceless and powerless. This disease has changed how we live and how we die. We are losing an unprecedented number of precious lives every day. We are not allowed to be there when our loved one breathes their last breath. We are not allowed to grieve together.

However, technology gives us options, and although they can't replace physical togetherness, they're better than nothing. I have talked to many people who have made good with a relative when they were on their death bed. Making good has taken a huge load off their shoulders, and for many people the current situation means they won't have the opportunity to do so.

But should we wait until the last moment? Anyone can pass away at any moment—heart attack, aneurysm, accident, and stroke are just a few examples that can cause sudden death.

I'm lucky in a way as I say what needs to be said—from my perspective. I've always been up-front with my relatives, and some of the words my mother or father told me when I was a teenager will always be with me:

"Treat the people around you the way you'd like to be treated."

"Treat your loved ones as if it were your last day with them."

"Concentrate on the living—there is nothing you can do for those who have passed."

While the last point has its validity, I only agree partially with it. Respectfully remembering those who are no longer with us can go a long way.

Thanking a person for something they have done is another task too many people leave for when their loved one is on his, her, or their deathbed. As already emphasized, this opportunity may never arise, so why not thank this person now? This can be a visit with a bunch of flowers and a box of chocolates to the auntie who taught you to distinguish toadstools from mushrooms or the uncle who covered up the evidence when you had raided your mum's cookie jar. It's always the time to make good.

I've been to a number of funerals, but I wasn't able to be at my mum's. She passed away in 1989 from breast cancer. I was 33 weeks pregnant with our first child and unfit for air travel. I remember the moment when the phone rang and my dad told me that Mum was no longer with us. We knew it was coming, but when it did happen, it was still overwhelming. Back then all we could do was think of her.

Twenty years of technological progress later, my husband and I were able to be at his mother's funeral—digitally. One of my sisters offered to ask the funeral celebrant whether she would allow her to put her mobile phone in front of her. We followed the proceedings from our home, sitting side by side, undistracted by the presence of other people, thoughts of whether we were wearing appropriate clothing or trying to identify people we had never seen before.

Once the proceedings had finished, we stayed where we were, reflecting on her life and just thinking of her, giving one another hugs and generally snuggling up.

Some ten years have passed since then, including my dad's funeral four years ago, which we experienced the same way as my mother-in-law's. Looking back now, I have no regrets about not having been there physically. The memories of them continue to live in our hearts.

So what's the essence of a funeral for me? It brings closure. It's part of the grieving process. The life of the person who has passed away is celebrated.

I only have positive memories of these two funerals we attended remotely. We didn't witness any jostling for the biggest piece of cake, no laughing, drinking, or exchanging of the latest gossip. We didn't have to put up with people who were only present in person, but not in spirit. It was quiet and thought-provoking. We wanted to be there, and that was all we cared about.

Looking back at my mum's funeral from which I have nothing—no closure, no memories—and comparing the two funerals we attended remotely with those I've been to in person, I can say that they rank equally in my memories of the person we lost. I have closure, I have the feeling that I was there—in spirit, and there have been no negative distractions, no negative thoughts caused by people who would have preferred to be somewhere else.

Not having a funeral service with loved ones present is a new aspect of our lives that may stay with us for the foreseeable future. We have to embrace the technology that enables us to at least get closure, which, for many, is the most important reason for having a funeral.

We can still grieve for the person and honour the person who died, in our thoughts and prayers.

It's up to us to not postpone to the last moment the things we know we should do. It's too late once the person is gone. If this has just happened to you, there is nothing that can be done in retrospect, but it can be the catalyst for sitting down and thinking about the loved ones who are still around. Make good with the people who matter to you, and don't hesitate to thank someone for what they have done for you. For if the unexpected happens, there will be one less weight left on your shoulders.

Stay Safe. Be Well.

Teresa Schreiber Werth

There is nothing to prove my claim. It's purely conjecture on my part, but prior to 9/11, I don't recall so many of us saying "I love you" before we hung up the phone or whenever we left the house, not just to our family, but to our friends as well. I remember the many news reports about people who were in the Twin Towers, making frantic phone calls to spouses, children, or parents as the World Trade Center buckled and crumbled and as an airplane was being taken over by heroic passengers before it crashed in Shanksville, Pennsylvania. So many voice mails were left with a final message of "I love you." In the days and weeks that followed that horrific day, I observed that many people around me were uttering those three little words *way more often* than I had ever heard them before. I remember at some point attributing this subtle, but obvious change to the effects of 9/11. Watching those tragic images over and over again, the tragedy was seared into our brains. We knew it wasn't just buildings that were destroyed. It was people—people with families whose hearts would be shattered. And so we had a collective moment of consciousness: *we need to tell them we love them again because we never know when it will be the last time.* And so we do—over and over again. Before we hang up the phone, as we leave the house, before we get on the

247

plane or train, or before we slam the car door, we tell the people who matter most that we love them. They already know it, but we need to remind them one more time, *just in case.*

I believe we've arrived at a new collective moment of consciousness. In nearly every e-mail I have received in March and April 2020, at the end of most phone calls from family, friends, or sometimes even strangers, I have heard some version of "Stay safe. Be well." There is no flashbulb moment like planes crashing into the World Trade Center to precipitate this response. The origin of this is much subtler.

When we first heard about the coronavirus, it was very far away, and we didn't feel threatened by it. But we watched it move across the continents on the nightly news until our "fight or flight" instinct began to kick in. That's when it became obvious that we couldn't outrun the virus, and we had nothing effective with which to fight it. The only effective way to stay safe was to treat *everyone* as if they had it and to act as if *we* had it ourselves. We needed to isolate ourselves, wear a mask and gloves, stay six feet away from others, disinfect everything, wash our hands repeatedly, and wait until a vaccine was found.

Then we learned that even people who showed no symptoms could be spreading the disease. So even those who were taking every precaution could somehow become infected with this deadly virus. Emotions ran from frustration to hypervigilance to denial to paranoia to disbelief and, for some, even indifference. At a time when science and data were clearly the ultimate sources of determining our course of action, the path forward was anything but clear.

That's when we began to hear this mantra of concern and hope: stay safe and be well. Because staying safe was not easy to do. You were susceptible to the consequences of other people's actions. And so you would try to stay safe by doing everything you could do, but would it be enough? And the wish for you to be well was a sincere hope that the virus wouldn't infect you, that you would be spared the physical assault of this disease and the many ways it could hurt you, from damaging your lungs and vital organs to causing your death.

I was sitting in the car the other day while my husband, wearing his mask, went into the drugstore to pick up a prescription. It was a very windy day. Just to the right of the front of our car, three seagulls were aloft, trying to fly. It was almost a surreal sight. They were suspended in air, flapping their wings and going absolutely nowhere. They were actually being held up by the wind, the same wind that was keeping them from going anywhere. It looked as if they were flying, but they weren't. I thought, *Poor honeys! I know just how you feel. I am going through the motions of everyday life: waking, showering, dressing, cooking, eating, and working (from home), but I'm actually going nowhere! And yet I need to do everything I can for me and my family to not get the coronavirus. I need to take all necessary precautions.*

We know it isn't just the economy that's been ravaged. It is people, people's businesses, jobs, health conditions, and families whose hearts are being shattered. And so we are having a collective moment of consciousness. Over and over again, spoken, written, prayed, thought, wished, and ordered: **STAY SAFE. BE WELL.**

I'm with You

Adam Lazarus

I see you.
I hear you.
I'm with you, my friends.

I'm there.
I support you.
And will 'til hate ends.

I'm watching.
And listening.
I'm taking it in.

I'm reading.
I'm learning.
I'm teaching my kin.

I'm standing.
I'm speaking.
I'm not staying silent.

I'm posting.
Protesting.
I'm peaceful, non-violent.

I'm caring.
I'm changing.
I'm challenging others.

I'm helping
And here for
My sisters and brothers.

I'm angry.
I'm active.
I accept. I'm all in!

Ending hate.
Fighting racism.
No more deaths due to skin!

Who's with me?
Who's fed up?
Who will enter this fight?

Don't sit there.
Do something.
Just do what is right!

I'm lucky.
I'm privileged.
This is not about me.

I know it.
I get it.
But we're stronger as "we".

I hear you.
I see you.
I'm an ally, my friends.

I'm behind you.
Forever.
Until racism ends.

Perseverance Is All I Know

Aylannie Campbell

In 2010, at the innocent age of seven years, I completed an activity in my classroom where students were asked to draw what we thought the world would look like in 2020. I drew things like cars driving on clouds, food falling from the sky, and people of all different colors holding hands. Ten years seemed so far away, yet in the blink of an eye, here we are. We are living in 2020, and there are no cars driving on clouds, *Cloudy with a Chance of Meatballs* is still just a fantasy movie, and unity and world peace are far from a reality. It is 2020, and things like slavery, racism, and segregation are still alive and steadily evolving. Yet my people and I continue to rise.

I am Aylannie Campbell, a 2020 graduate of EJ Wilson High School in Spencerport, New York. I spent the entirety of my high-school career doing everything in my power to ensure that no Black child will move through this school system or grow up in this community feeling as belittled, dismissed, and unheard as I did for these past 13 years. Diversity was absent, and equity was lacking.

I constantly felt that, as one of just a few Black or brown students in any classroom, I might as well have been the pink elephant in the room. Teachers and students alike saw the color of my skin and were absolutely blind to what it meant to be Black in a predominantly white school. I consistently experienced more hate than acceptance. Perseverance became my standard response. Perseverance was all I knew.

I heard racial slurs in my classrooms and watched my teachers look the other way. At only six years old, I was alienated on the playground because of the color of my skin. For more than five years, I straightened my curls and gave in to assimilation because I was convinced that there was a definition of beauty that I did not match. These experiences were and are traumatizing, damaging for anyone to go through. My school days were certainly not ideal encounters for a child—any child—and especially for a child so visibly different.

To be Black in America is to be resilient. The evil and hate I experienced growing up have shaped me into being the resilient and powerful young woman I am today, determined to make history—positive history, radical history, and unapologetic history. In the same high school where I felt marginalized because I was underrepresented, I took it upon myself to run for positions in student council, to join committees, and to speak on panels addressing issues of social and racial justice and culturally responsible education. I refused to be silenced. I refused to be dismissed, and despite every obstacle, I held my head up high and pursued my legacy for the sake of all the younger kids coming up who look like me.

America today is battling two deadly pandemics—racism and COVID-19. In spite of the ways these viruses are disproportionately killing Black, Indigenous, and People of Color (BIPOC), we continue to rise. After the deaths of Ahmaud Arbery, Breonna Taylor, George Floyd, and Rayshard Brooks, our country is experiencing an exponential, powerful resurgence of the Black Lives Matter movement. A movement that has been around for years is now getting the attention it deserves, and long-awaited change is, hopefully, on the horizon. Though this effort has been a marathon and not a sprint, such division and disease have brought a new wave of hope through unity as hundreds of people, from all backgrounds, ethnicities, and skin colors, join forces to bring about this long-awaited change. Unfortunately, after over 400 years of battling oppression as well as systemic and institutional racism, oppressed people everywhere still have so much work to do.

Spencerport High School's student organization DASH2Change (Declare Action 2 Shift Humanity) has been a safe space for many students who look like me. This group was established about four years ago in my high school as part of a youth summit, ROC2Change. It has evolved into a safe place for people of all colors to celebrate diversity, share similar stories, and work toward common goals for societal change. I am hopeful this club will continue conversations regarding diversity, equality, equity, and social justice with future generations of Spencerport students.

In June of 2020, a Black Lives Matter rally was held in my hometown. It was hosted by Spencerport alumni and DASH2Change. Despite the town's population being 93 percent white and the rally taking place during the pandemic, the community came out. An attentive mask-wearing, sign-carrying, mostly white crowd came out to listen, to learn, and to discuss. The same community founded on white privilege, gentrification, genocide, and generational wealth came out *as allies* to amplify the voices of the unheard. Because of them I have hope.

Message from a 2020 Graduate

A Baccalaureate Address
Camryn Zeitvogel

I think it is safe to say that the coronavirus is at the forefront of everyone's minds. From constant news feeds showing fear-inducing reports to constant debates over masks and physical distancing, everyone is starting to feel on edge. Although many of the current precautions being taken are designed for the short term, I think that there will be long-lasting effects stemming from the COVID-19 outbreak.

As far as society is concerned, the economy is already suffering. Unemployment has reached the same levels that were present during the Great Depression, and the FED is buying more stocks than it has in over a decade to try to save the economy. Even when the United States and other dominant countries start reopening, it will take years to repair the damage. The job loss in America will not just go away; many businesses, large and small, have lost significant amounts of money and customers and will no longer be able to support as many employees as they had before even when the pandemic is over. Everyone will have to work hard to make ends meet, but people who were already financially unstable will suffer the most, including students like myself. Not only are colleges rapidly losing money, but they also aren't even sure they will be able to reopen in the fall.

Across some states, budget cuts into the next fiscal year are already being made, including cuts to education. The economic fallout alone is enough to scare anyone into making drastic changes just to cope.

As concerning as the failing economy is, there is another long-term effect that is even scarier: the mental health impact. There have already been suicides as a result of social isolation. The human spirit was never meant to be alone. The lack of usual interactions like hugging has left many people feeling more alone than ever. Studies on the effects of loneliness on the human spirit have already proven that loneliness is a silent killer. Although it affects everyone, I think that students are suffering from this the most. Children need school not only for the academics, but for learning social skills. Today's children are already at a disadvantage because of the rise of online communication. In addition to this, young people need outlets. When the brain is not yet fully developed, it is more difficult to cope with problems and emotions. Students need things like recess, sports, clubs, and other activities to channel their feelings and energy in a healthy way. Because of the COVID-19 situation, students of all ages and all backgrounds are suffering. Some are even dying tragic, preventable deaths because they were unable to have access to their biggest support system: school. Many students, from kindergarten all the way through twelfth grade, rely on connections to their peers, teachers, and coaches not only for academic or extracurricular instruction, but also for emotional and spiritual support.

Personally, I was very close with many of my teachers. Without the support I am used to having from my teachers, loneliness has essentially become my closest friend. I, as well as the rest of the class of 2020, will never get our senior year back. We will never get to play our last games on the home turf nor perform our last shows in our high-school auditoriums. We will never get the same kind of closure that our older friends had and our younger friends will someday have. It feels like a complete injustice. There is pain, suffering, and hurting everywhere in the United States and around the globe because of COVID-19. But despite how broken many people feel, there are still lessons to be learned. There is still hope to be felt, and there are still acts of God to be witnessed.

The first and, perhaps, most obvious one is the class of 2020. The class of 2020 is going to be remembered like no other. I suspect that someday down the road, we will all be attending our various class reunions, having better attendance than any other class because we will have a special bond that they never had. If there is one thing I have learned from my personal high-school experience, it is that shared suffering will unite people like nothing else. My class will be united because we went through this together. We all lost something or someone together. No one has been spared from this, but at the same time, I have to believe that God will not forsake us and that this will bring so many of us together. In some ways, it already has.

Different trends that came from the pandemic have already brought us together. I see it when the children in my neighborhood draw chalk hearts on the sidewalk. I see it when a parade of cars drive through my neighborhood for someone's birthday. I see it when there are 300 people logged in to online church. I see it when musicians are offering free lessons to students who have lost access to their private teachers. I see it in all the employees, from teachers to nurses to grocery store cashiers and beyond, who are doing their absolute best in the worst situations. Suffering does bring unity; we just have to open our eyes to see it.

The second glimmer of light I have seen through all this is gratitude. I can admit, I would have been the first to complain about my life before all this happened. I felt like I had nothing. Although this has been arguably the worst way to learn it, I have learned that I have so many blessings in my life. I have learned that it is 100 percent true when they say, "You don't know what you've got until it's gone." If any part of me is going to be permanently changed because of COVID-19, the quarantine, and the loss of my senior year, it's going to be the amount of time I spend counting my blessings. Although I can't promise I'll never complain again or never take anything for granted again, I can promise that I will catch myself doing those things. I was so fortunate before, and I continue to be fortunate even now when things aren't so great. I think many people would agree with me, too. I think this has been a major wake-up call for all of us who are learning that just because life isn't perfect doesn't mean there is nothing to be grateful for. There is *always* something. If there was ever a time to lean on God, it's now. If there was ever a time to actively count your blessings, it's now. What do we have to lose at this point? I'd say, not much. If there was ever a time to reflect, this is it. And I think if we all look hard enough, we'll find positive changes mixed in among all the tragedy.

To Propagate a Home

Ayanna Woods

We must have uncommon strength to face the wound
and refuse to let it wither.

We must have uncommon faith to plunge our hands into the land
and nurture an abundant place.

They say it's a lost cause—
They haven't seen the new roots
Weaving through the dark.

They say it isn't worth it—
They haven't watched with joy
As each new bud emerges

When they cut off a branch that they say is dying,
It takes uncommon faith to grow.

These roots have never forgotten
How to grab hold of the soil.

This branch has never forgotten
How to reach up toward the sky.

No Man Is an Island

Ryan R. Tebo

Is our world on fire? Have we lost all control over our own circumstances? Right now, the answer to both of these questions seems to be an emphatic, "Yes!" With the stress of the pandemic stretching society and individuals to a razor-thin perseverance and the justified rage against institutionalized racial injustice and police violence reaching a critical mass and erupting across the country, America has reached its tipping point. At this moment in time, WB Yeats's "The Second Coming" seems like a prophecy fulfilled:

> Things fall apart; the centre cannot hold;
> Mere anarchy is loosed upon the world,
> The blood-dimmed tide is loosed, and everywhere
> The ceremony of innocence is drowned.[3]

For the foreseeable future, we can expect more and more of this uncertainty and turbulence to directly and profoundly affect each of

---

[3]   William Butler Yeats, "The Second Coming," https://www.poetryfoundation.org/poems/43290/the-second-coming.

our lives. To not expect this risks a tragic naivete we cannot afford. So many of us feel like, as individuals, we have no center to hold on to; we are taken by the tide out to the merciless sea, alone and drowning.

A decade ago, I almost drowned while wading at a beach in Maine after being pulled off the shoreline by a strong riptide, violently separated from my friend who had been standing next to me. Those minutes being dragged under the sea, with each new, rapidly occurring wave, seemed like an eternity. Luckily, I managed to keep breathing long enough to survive until the onslaught of waves ceased, and I finally found firm sand under my now-trembling legs. We are in the throes of a global riptide, fighting for our lives and our sanity. But the crucial thing is that, unlike when I nearly drowned, now we are not alone even if only virtually.

Having emerged alive from the Atlantic Ocean ten years ago, I then flew back over it to permanently settle in Stockholm, Sweden. Being separated from family and witnessing from afar (on social media) their home country being ripped apart are difficult for every expatriate. Feelings of hopelessness, frustration, and guilt can become overwhelming. My particular situation is, however, a bit surreal. As Stockholm is embraced by a budding summer warmth, people are flocking to parks and outdoor café seating, enjoying the sun, and apparently ignoring the pandemic. While the international reports of Swedish life having returned to normal are grossly exaggerated, it does feel, relatively speaking, more normal here. That being said, I have been teaching online and rarely leaving my apartment, aside from taking my dog for walks or occasionally meeting a friend for a walk outside. The routines of regular life have, even here, largely screeched to a halt.

Without these routines and living far away from family can lead expatriates especially to feel desperately isolated. This is also a reality recognized by many who still live in their hometown. However, expatriates deal with these feelings in addition to the already present anxieties and alienation of being immigrants, and they often do not have the same support networks more likely existing for them in their home country. When things fall apart like this, we feel isolated, alone, helpless, and unable to have any control over our realities. For me, the key is turning away from the staunch individualism we, as a society, have so completely espoused, especially since the 1980s. Instead, our best hope is to do everything in our power to turn toward solidarity and empathy. This is really the only way we can survive, as individuals and as a society, given the daunting challenges we face now and in the future. John Donne's famous argument against self-isolationism, "No man is an island," speaks to me strongly at this moment:

> Any man's death diminishes me,
> because I am involved in mankind.
> And therefore never send to know for whom
> the bell tolls; it tolls for thee.[4]

This is why I, separated by an ocean, feel outrage at the death of George Floyd and why you should too. This is why I look to find any way I can to be more involved in mankind despite the restrictive circumstances (or because of them). This is why I can feel less alone and

---

4 John Donne, "No Man Is an Island," http://www.luminarium.org/sevenlit/donne/meditation17.php.

isolated. I wish there were more I could do for my family and friends back in America. But empathy and solidarity stretch across the globe, and these are the most important things to send back home.

We can still be a part of building communities, building hope, and building a sustainable future (ecologically and socially). And when you reach out your hand to help others, to commune with others, and to build new communities with others, you will find that it is not just other people whom you are helping. You are also helping yourself to be less isolated, less alone, and more prepared to meet an uncertain future. This reaching out is something we can control and sometimes may be the only thing. Fostering empathy and solidarity is the most profound way we can give our lives the new meaning we so desperately need.[5]

---

[5] Ryan Tebo was hospitalized in Sweden with COVID-19 and treated in the hospital there for three days in October 2020. He has fully recovered.

Empathy

Mara Sapon-Shevin

One of the gifts of the pandemic has been my growing empathy.
I have always thought I was empathic and would hope my friends
would say so, but having grown up in a family in which "bad" feel-
ings were corrected, I know I have also been judgmental.
So now
I have increased empathy for people who are lonely. The person who
lingers too long or talks too much or too fast, trying to extend the
conversation.
Because that is me also.
And I have increased empathy for people who are anxious or fearful,
seeing risk or danger that others don't, or won't name or acknowledge.
Because that is me also.
And I have increased empathy for people who are sad, overwhelmed
by hopelessness and despair.
Because that is me also.
So, my deep support for anyone who experiences loneliness or anxi-
ety or sadness or depression.
I get it more deeply now.
I apologize for any spoken or even unspoken judgments I have made.

We Can't Let a Good Crisis Go to Waste

Andrew Penn

How do we navigate our grief? We must first find a place to sit with that which is broken. This is going to be a slow and difficult journey. How can we fortify ourselves for the long night ahead? I offer some pragmatic notions that may help to build a vessel to hold our grief. They will not all be useful or useful for everyone, but perhaps, they are of use to some as they have been for me.

- We will need to create *new rituals and routines* even if they are as simple as a daily walk around the block. We may benefit from planning the first part of the next day before we go to bed so that we can create momentum in the new day.
- *Meditation* allows us the space to notice our thoughts and feelings without having to act upon them.
- *Keep the body moving:* We need exercise now more than ever for our physical and mental well-being.
- *Get outside:* Fresh air, sunshine, and an open sky are medicine.

- *Pay attention to our inner worlds as much as we do the news or social media.*
- *Appreciate beauty:* You don't need to be an artist to appreciate the flowers in your neighbor's garden or a beautiful sunset when out on a walk.
- *Stay connected:* Infection control calls for *physical* distancing. We can still be *socially connected.*
- *Find opportunities for gratitude:* Can we find moments to savor and appreciate?
- *Practice compassion:* This is difficult. And we're all going through it together. How can we be kinder to one another?

Finally, we are called to make space for our grief in whatever form that takes. There will be times when we want none of this, when our hearts are heavy with all that we have lost, both large and small, that the suggestions on this list just feel like another opportunity for failure. There are times when we will want to weep and other times when we want to sit and stare plaintively out the window. If that is what your soul is asking for in that moment, allow it that too. TS Elliot ended his poem "The Waste Land" with the haunting line, "These fragments I have shored against my ruins." This time will undoubtedly leave us both brokenhearted and greater of spirit. There is room for it all if we can allow it.

Acceptance and Meaning

Awaiting us is the process of acceptance (the 5th stage) and finding meaning (the 6th stage) in our loss. How do we begin to imagine accepting sick-

ness, disruption, and death, or even more, finding meaning in it?

We each must find our own meaning from this event. This is a
process that will take time, introspection, and community. And even
when we find the meaning, it will remain a poor substitute for that
which we have lost. We will be called upon to experience all that we
don't have bandwidth to feel right now. For those who have unexpectedly lost loved ones and who could not be with them in their
last moments because of fear of contamination, this pain will be even
greater. To be sure, we are experiencing a trauma, as a society, and
for many of us, before this is all over, a personal one. Our grief will
be felt both individually and collectively and we will need to mourn
both as individuals, but also as a community. Grief is not meant to
be navigated alone, but rather to be held in the soul of the village in
ritual and remembrance, however we define that.

Post-traumatic stress arises, in part, when our <u>assumptions of
safety in a benevolent world have been shattered</u>. I suspect that the
return to our new form of normal, whatever that looks like, will be a
reversal of the process through which we took up defenses against the
virus—only much slower. While we may ache for a return of public
life, we will likely come out of our shells gradually. What will it be
like when we can gather again, to fly on a plane, or to shake the hand
of a new friend? Will we ever shake hands again? Or will we regard
everyone with the vague suspicion that has befallen us now, where all
at once, the threat seems omnipresent and yet nowhere to be found?
And what if, in the absence of a vaccine, we have flare-ups of infection? Our response to a renewed threat may be excessive or disorga-
nized, as can be expected from a population that is traumatized.

Fortunately, we know from the post-traumatic stress literature that humans are incredibly resilient. The vast majority of people who experience trauma do not go on to develop post-traumatic stress disorder (PTSD). This is the good news. Even better news is that some can come out of the experience stronger.

To do this, a certain amount of engagement with our loss is essential. While brooding over the trauma is not helpful, thoughtful, purpose-driven reflection can move us towards an experience of meaning and resolution. Traits such as optimism, acceptance, and a search for meaning support the post-traumatic growth process on an individual level, while social support, spiritual groups, and community engagement support healing the larger whole.

The biggest mistake we could make is to try to return to things as they were without first examining if the changed world is actually a better world. We must not let a perfectly good crisis go to waste.

As both people and a collective society, we continue to ask the question "How could we be better?" How can we acknowledge the essential lesson of this virus, that we are all vulnerable and we are all connected? And if we are all connected, how can we be more humane and just with each other? How do we create a society in which health is the foundation of our wealth and that we create structures to ensure the well-being for all of its members? No longer can we see the health of our neighbors as a silo that is separate from our own. When one member of the village gets sick, we all suffer. As we turn our attention to our personal lives, we are asked if we wish to return to the same frantic pace that was exhausting many of us before it suddenly, unexpectedly ground to a halt. We have been shocked into asking, "What is important to you? What *really* matters?"

(This article is excerpted from three blog posts: "The Six Phases of Grief During Covid-19" by Andrew Penn, MS, NP, PMHNP-BC, March 24, 2020, https://www.psychcongress.com/blogger/andrew-penn-rn-ms-np-cns-aprn-bc.)

The story ends,
another starts,
inviting
transformation.
Every choice we make today
creates the living chapter
that passes on and offers hope—
or not—to those who follow;
We will adapt; we will endure;
we will survive this illness;
and we will add our wisdom
to stories shining light.

(From *Candles in the Dark* by Kitty O'Meara
The-Daily-Round.com, April 9, 2020
Used with kind permission.)

Epilogue

When I first started to think about finding writers who would join me in creating this book, we were living in a world facing global climate and pollution crises so extreme that the canals of Venice were mostly devoid of fish, people in India had not been able to see the Himalayas for over 30 years, a visible smog blanketed large cities like Los Angeles, and asthma rates skyrocketed in the Bronx. We literally couldn't breathe in many places on earth. Scientists had been predicting a global pandemic would come, and sure enough, between late 2019 and 2020, we watched the novel coronavirus spread around the world.

The pandemic led to a health-care crisis for which we were not, in any way, prepared. There were no scientific or institutional plans for dealing with it. Shortages of every necessary commodity made our response woefully slow and inadequate. We couldn't breathe because we were afraid of inhaling the microorganism that could sicken or kill us. We couldn't breathe because of the masks we were required to wear.

Strategic use of isolation and social distancing created an economic pandemic. Our economy tanked as we lost jobs, businesses, savings, and other basic forms of security. We could not breathe as we watched unimaginable things happen in our lives, our communities and our nation revealing the horrific scope of social disparities in our country. Our elders were disproportionately dying in nursing homes. Infection and death rates soared in prisons and detention centers, in indigenous communities, in Black and brown communities, among our refugee population, and in poor neighborhoods everywhere.

And then we watched *another* Black person suffocated to death by police despite his repeated protests, saying "I can't breathe." That moment, now inextricably linked to COVID-19, informed us of America's undeniable historical disparities rooted in white, capitalistic, and patriarchal structures.

Suddenly, the whole world can't breathe. The unfolding crisis isn't about one pandemic; it is about *four pandemics:* COVID-19, climate change, the crumbling economy, and historic/systemic racial injustice. These events, taken together, demand that we ask ourselves what kind of world we want and what kind of people we want to be. Our unwillingness to act decisively *now* will result in the breath being sucked out of everything we claim to value.

There is a tremendous amount of work to be done to save ourselves and our planet. The first step requires each of us to recognize and affirm these problems. The next step is to believe we each *must* play a part in creating the necessary changes. And finally, as we reflect on the stories so honestly and bravely told in these pages about where we find ourselves in 2020, we each must commit to being *an intentional part* of the very changes we desire. This work, this change, is only possible if we do it *with* one another *for* one another.

Micky ScottBey Jones says it prophetically in Invitation to Brave Space:

> Together we will create *brave space*
> Because there is no such thing as "safe space"
> We exist in the real world
> We all carry scars and we have all caused wounds.
> In this space
> We seek to turn down the volume of the outside world,
> We amplify voices that fight to be heard elsewhere,
> We call each other to more truth and love
> We have the right to start somewhere and continue to grow.
> We have the responsibility to examine what we think we know.
> We will not be perfect.
> This space will not be perfect.
> It will not always be what we wish it to be
> But
> It will be *our brave space together,*
> *And*
> *We will work on it side by side.*

Teresa Schreiber Werth
Rochester, New York, June 2020

Slivers of Light

Our present challenges and suffering are nothing
new. Disorienting, yes. And for many, exhausting
and terrifying and lonely and agonizingly painful. But regardless of what one believes about the
divine, it's clear there's something—call it a spirit
or a thread or a bridge or a twisty tie—that links
us together through miles and centuries. We
don't have to fathom it to feel it.

—Elizabeth Alexander

Yes, we're feeling a number of different griefs.
We feel the world has changed, and it has. We
know this is temporary, but it doesn't feel that
way, and we realize things will be different. Just
as going to the airport is forever different from
how it was before 9/11, things will change and
this is the point at which they changed. The loss
of normalcy; the fear of economic toll; the loss of
connection. This is hitting us and we're grieving.

Collectively. We are not used to this kind of collective grief in the air.

—David Kessler

Hope is being able to see that there is light despite all of the darkness.

—Desmond Tutu

The most authentic thing about us is our capacity to create, to overcome, to endure, to transform, to love and to be greater than our suffering.

—Ben Okri

We are all just walking each other home.

—Ram Dass

Start where you are. Use what you have. Do what you can.

—Arthur Ashe

Veterans of past epidemics have long warned that American society is trapped in a cycle of panic and neglect. When a "new normal" sets in, the abnormal once again becomes unimaginable.

—Ed Yong

We don't realize how alone we are or have been until we find the right time, place or person to release those emotions. Which is why the emotional stress level of this pandemic is so high and not well understood. It is triggering every trauma we've ever experienced in this life and before—what we call implicit vs explicit memories because they are stored so deep in our DNA we feel them but we don't remember them. Be gentle with yourself as you move through a new phase of your healing and embrace it for its releasing power.

—Grandmother Turtlekneader

One of the most calming and powerful actions you can do to intervene in a stormy world is to stand up and show your soul. Soul on deck shines like gold in dark times. The light of the soul throws sparks, can send up flares, builds signal fires...causes proper matters to catch fire... Struggling souls catch light from other souls who are fully lit and willing to show it. If you would help to calm the tumult, this is one of the strongest things you can do. Do not lose heart. We were made for these times.

—Clarissa Pinkola Estés

A clarion call for courageous action beckons. How do we answer? How do we find the grit to continue despite our fears, to be our best selves, and to get ourselves through this predicament that we're all in together? What story will be told of these challenging days?

—Andrew Penn

They are us and we are them
human beings in search of joy, love,
security, respect, health, peace of mind.
and when they are diminished,
when they are lost,
we are all lost and diminished.
We should all be outraged.
We should all be determined
to make the world safe for
human beings

—ALL HUMAN BEINGS—

No exceptions.

—Spiritmover

Why wear a mask? Out of respect. When you wear a mask you are saying, I respect my neighbors. When you wear a mask you are saying, I respect nurses and doctors. When you wear a mask you are saying, I respect other people. We all need to show respect to one another in difficult times. Wearing a face covering is a small inconvenience to protect others. We have gotten through this crisis by standing together and doing the right thing. The right thing—the respectful thing—is to wear a mask.

—NYS Governor Andrew Cuomo

Storytelling has the ability to conjure the deepest parts of ourselves and reimagine time and thus reimagine hope. Storytelling allows us to embrace what is far away, remember what was forgotten, and hope for a future existing now.

—Jake Skeets

My humanity is bound up in yours, for we can only be human together.

—Desmond Tutu

We wait, knowing that when this is over
A lot of us—not all perhaps—but most,
Will be slightly different people,
And our world, though diminished,
Will be much bigger, its beauty revealed afresh.

—Alexander McCall Smith

I see you. I hear you. I stand with you. I stand with those seeking justice and equality. Those that are risking everything in order to change the racial divide. We come together as human beings, sharing this earth, seeking what is right.

—Ed Gonzalez

There is no "one size fits all" answer when it comes to human beings, there are however, some "one size fits all" principles we can strive to achieve: to love and care for one another and to think before reacting.

—Kit Miller, MK Gandhi
Institute for Nonviolence

I share this music, which has helped shape the evolution of my life, with the hope that it might spark a conversation about how culture can be a source of the solutions we need. It is one more experiment, this time a search for answers to the question: What can we can do together, that we cannot do alone?

—Yo-Yo Ma,
cellist, Bach Cello Suites, 5/24/20

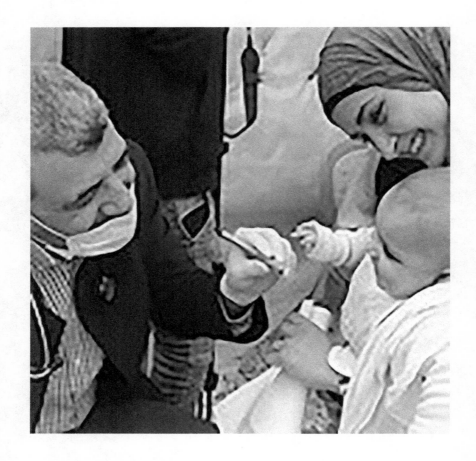

Proceeds from the sale of this book will be donated to the Society of Refugee Healthcare Providers, a U.S. nonprofit organization dedicated to improving the health care of refugees and asylum seekers as well as addressing equity in health care (www.refugeesociety.org).

Society of Refugee
Healthcare Providers

A Message from James Sutton, PA-C:

Mahatma Gandhi once said "The true measure of any society can be found in how it treats its most vulnerable members."

Even though we can all verbalize who we think are vulnerable members of our society, few would disagree that resettled refugees and asylum seekers—especially children—comprise our most vulnerable. Fleeing war, violence, and ethnic cleansing, these people run for their lives to seek refuge in our country. They are our neighbors; our new fellow citizens. As the lyrics on the accompanying page so aptly state: I can never truly see the world through your eyes or take away your pain, but I'm listening...

We not only have an obligation to listen, but more importantly, to be a voice for those that don't have a voice. The proceeds from this book will be donated to a non-profit organization that gives that voice. The Society of Refugee Healthcare Providers stands up and supports these vulnerable patients by educating physicians, nurses, social workers and resettlement workers about the best way to deliver medical care for refugees and asylum seekers. Through our efforts, these vulnerable members of our society can receive access to quality healthcare that allows them to heal from their trauma and start a new life in our community.

If you think about it... We are all refugees. The United States was formed and built by immigrants. Unless you are a full-blooded Native American, all your ancestors were immigrants seeking refuge in a new land. We now have an opportunity to give back and help these newest members of our society. We can help them thrive, show them they are loved, lift them up, and celebrate their acculturation into our society.

The Society of Refugee Healthcare Providers thanks you for helping us help them.

No Other People's Children

Elizabeth Alexander

How did we get to this place
Where we could look at each other's face
And see anything but beauty and understanding?
I want to know who you are,
And face the suffering that keeps us far apart
I can never truly see the world through your eyes
Or take away your pain,
But I'm listening, and I'm hoping you can hear me saying:

You are my neighbor. You are beloved.
You are worth seeing for who you are.
You are my neighbor. You are beloved.
You are worth seeing for who you are.
I'm here, I'm listening, I'm here listening with you:

Break bread with me.
Make peace with me.
Speak the truth with me.
Begin again with me.
Relate with me.

Create with me.

Be the change with me

That keeps our children safe and free:

There are no other people's heartaches.

There are no other people's injuries.

There are no other people's children in this world.

See what is unseen,

Say what is unspoken,

Believe that there's no wall between our beating hearts.

Hold hands with me.

Forgive with me.

Make mistakes with me,

And take a chance with me.

Be whole with me.

Be real with me.

Start to heal with me

So we can live courageously.

There are no other people's heartaches.

There are no other people's injuries.

There are no other people's children in this world.

To listen go to:

https://soundcloud.com/songcrafterliz/no-other-peoples-children-1-4-part-choir-and-piano-1

Image List

Don Werth, cover image

Barbara Barrows, p. 36

Ursula Roma, p. 44

Gina Marie Griffee: p. 48

Adam A. Werth: p. 54

lionalert.org: p. 56

Paul Barrows: p. 60

mhpsalud.org: p.64

Mara Ahmed: p. 76

Gloria Osborne: p.84

MUSE website: p. 90

Francis DiPonzio: MD Sutton p. 112

Maria Delgado Sutton: p. 116

Miguel & Delia: MD Sutton: p. 128

"Hamilton" @ London Correctional, Ohio: p. 134

Guy Banks @ London Correctional, Ohio: p. 140

Laura Bascomb: p. 150

Katie Myers: p. 156

Brian & Jeanee Linden: p. 166

affordablecomfort.org: p. 172

Gloria Osborne: p. 178

Laura Young Photography: p. 182

Steve McAlpin: p. 188

Lauren Benton: p. 206

Babak Tafreshi: p. 212

Liza Donovan: p. 216

Jean Junker & Colton: Barbara Whittemore: p. 222

EVOKIST Photography Columbus Statue Indigenous People: p. 230

Careers.gov.nz: p. 246

Aylannie Campbell: p. 254

Camryn Zeitvogel: p. 258

Original print, Mabel Lawson: p. 268

Empathy.com: p. 274

Pixabay image 20237: p. 282

Adam A. Werth: p. 284

UKIM- Mobile Healthcare Camps for Syrian Refugees 2017: p. 296

Adam A. Werth, back cover: corona flower bouquet

All other pictures/images are from the editor's private collection.

Additional References

Amanda Gorman.com Wordsmith. Changemaker. The youngest inaugural poet in U.S. history, as well as an award-winning writer and cum laude graduate of Harvard University. She has written for the *New York Times* and has three books forthcoming.

calm.com Calm's mission is to make the world happier and healthier. Calm is a meditation, sleep and relaxation app dedicated to introducing our world-wide Calm Community to the amazing benefits of mindfulness.

cardthartic.com Exceptional greeting cards for all occasions, including sentiments specific to emotions and issues related to the pandemic and beyond.

gratefulness.org Discover the nourishing and transformative power of living gratefully—available to you within every moment of your life—through the offerings on this website and the warm heart of our global community.

grief.com Help for grief because love never dies, offering books, videos, and support resources.

headspace.com Guided meditations, animations, articles and videos.

inspiredtogive.org The basis of InspiredtoGive.org is to encourage and document acts of good that are evident in kindness, respect, courage, reconciliation and transformation, shared by individuals and organizations, day-in and day-out. It is a practice of truth-sharing and good-giving that unites us, prepares and strengthens us to shape the future with optimism and expectation of progress. There is no political or religious agenda, no hidden manipulation. Honestly, it's an agenda for truth and goodwill.

inspiremore.com Our vision since day one has always been to build a business that taps into our deep human desire to be inspired and to inspire others with the goal of making the world a better place.

johnpavlovitz.com John Pavlovitz is a writer, pastor, and activist from Wake Forest, NC. A 25-year veteran in the trenches of local church ministry, John is committed to equality, diversity, and justice—both inside and outside faith communities, and actively working for a more compassionate planet.

refugeingrief.com I'm Megan, a psychotherapist, writer, grief advocate, & communication expert dedicated to helping you live through things you never thought you'd face. I'm proud to have created an online community and resource that helps people survive some of the hardest experiences of their lives. Through my book, podcasts, and online courses, I help people learn the skills they need to love themselves—and each other—better.

reimagine.org We help individuals and communities apply spiritual wisdom to everyday life by (1) Awakening Imagination; (2) Creating Practical Content; (3) Facilitating Experiential Learning; and (4) Empowering Leaders who can teach others.

rememberingalife.com Your guide to honoring a life well-lived, from planning a tribute to mourning a loved one.

speakinggrief.org Speaking Grief is a public media initiative aimed at creating a more grief-aware society by validating the experience of grievers and helping to guide those who wish to support them.

the-daily-round.com For 25 years, Kitty O'Meara and her husband have lived at Full Moon Cottage, with the 4-legged companions who have always blessed their lives. She has worked as a teacher, and as a spiritual care provider in hospital and hospice settings, and has always been a writer. She started her blog in 2011 and shared her short essays, poetry, and photography for years, before moving on to other pursuits and some necessary healing. The coming of this current pandemic led her to compose a piece she called "In the Time of Pandemic," that she posted for friends, on Facebook. Ironically, during a pandemic, it went viral, as "And the People Stayed Home." She resumed writing her blog, and the poem has led to many artistic collaborations as well as a children's book with a publisher who has contracted more books with O'Meara. The poem was also included in the poetry anthology: *Together in a Sudden Strangeness: America's Poets Respond to the Pandemic*, edited by Alice Quinn.

https://gandhiinstitute.org/ Gandhi Institute for Non-Violence: Our Mission is to help individuals and communities develop the inner resources and practical skills needed to achieve a nonviolent, sustainable, and just world.

thekindnessrocksproject.com One message, at just the right moment, can change someone's entire day, outlook, life.

About the Editor

Teresa Schreiber Werth is a retired communications professional, freelance writer, author, editor and certified funeral and wedding celebrant. Her initial efforts in creating this book focused on addressing the needs of families whose loved ones were dying alone. Werth soon realized that the scope of the pandemic was a prism of challenges and suffering, experienced by diverse communities in diverse ways. Through an extended network of creative and generous people, she sought essays, memoirs, and poems based on both professional insight and lived experiences. Writers of all ages and a variety of backgrounds and nationalities responded enthusiastically to her invitation.

Learn more online at www.thedandelionbook.com.

CPSIA information can be obtained
at www.ICGtesting.com
Printed in the USA
BVHW080316040921
615860BV00001B/3

9 781662 424694